BRIGHT NOTES

MY ANTONIA AND OTHER WORKS BY WILLA CATHER

Intelligent Education

Nashville, Tennessee

BRIGHT NOTES: My Antonia and Other Works
www.BrightNotes.com

No part of this publication may be used or reproduced in any manner whatsoever without written permission, except in the case of brief quotations in critical articles and reviews. For permissions, contact Influence Publishers http://www.influencepublishers.com.

ISBN: 978-1-645425-36-6 (Paperback)
ISBN: 978-1-645425-37-3 (eBook)

Published in accordance with the U.S. Copyright Office Orphan Works and Mass Digitization report of the register of copyrights, June 2015.

Originally published by Monarch Press.
Joan T. Nourse; Robin Fleisig, 1964
2020 Edition published by Influence Publishers.

Interior design by Lapiz Digital Services. Cover Design by Thinkpen Designs.

Printed in the United States of America.

Library of Congress Cataloging-in-Publication Data forthcoming.
Names: Intelligent Education
Title: BRIGHT NOTES: My Antonia and Other Works
Subject: STU004000 STUDY AIDS / Book Notes

CONTENTS

1)	Introduction to Willa Cather	1
2)	Introduction to My Antonia	10
3)	Textual Analysis	11
	Book I: The Shimerdas - Chapters 1-8	11
	Book I: The Shimerdas - Chapters 9-15	24
	Book II: The Hired Girls - Chapters 1-7	38
	Book II: The Hired Girls - Chapters 8-15	52
	Book III: Lena Lingard	66
	Book IV: The Pioneer Woman's Story	80
	Book V: Cuzak's Boys	95
4)	Character Analyses	106
5)	Critical Commentary	116
6)	Review Questions and Answers	121
7)	O Pioneers!	130
8)	The Song of the Lark	134

9)	One of Ours	140
10)	Death Comes for the Archbishop	142
11)	Topics for Further Research	144
12)	Bibliography	145

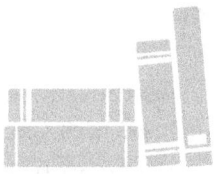

INTRODUCTION TO WILLA CATHER

THE POSITIVE VIEW

Some modern writers are pessimistic about man's power to achieve true greatness in a world that often seems chaotic. In her novels and stories, Willa Cather was one twentieth-century author who continually reaffirmed a belief that even against great odds the human spirit could triumph. Few difficulties, she thought, were insurmountable if an individual had vision and determination.

EARLY DAYS IN NEBRASKA

As a creative artist she drew heavily upon her personal experiences. Many of these were such as to support her faith in the capacity of human beings to endure much and heroically persevere. Born in 1873 in Virginia, she moved with her parents nine years later to rural Nebraska. All around her there in the 1880s she saw courageous settlers breaking ground, building homes, braving extremes of climate, and finally becoming prosperous farmers. Not all, of course, succeeded. Some lost heart and gave up. Nevertheless, the wild Divide was being tamed, and brave men and women were doing it.

Among them she respected most highly the immigrant pioneers, who started with so little and could not even speak the language. Exploring the countryside on her pony, she made friends with many of the Bohemians, Germans, and Scandinavians in the area. She was interested in their unusual customs and native dishes, and she noted admiringly how they worked hard, paid off mortgages, and raised fine big families. These sturdy, indomitable people she was later to immortalize in *O Pioneers*! and *My Antonia*.

REACTIONS TO RED CLOUD

After two years her family moved again, this time into the nearby town of Red Cloud. There in a rather crowded house, Willa lived with her brothers and sisters until 1890, when she left for college. Red Cloud, founded only thirteen years before, was then a busy railroad center with bright prospects. Here the girl could not help hearing of those daring and enterprising individuals responsible for getting the tracks laid across miles and miles of grassy plains. She pays tribute to these men of vision in her portrait of Captain Forrester in *A Lost Lady*.

Other aspects of Red Cloud, however, she found less agreeable. Some townsfolk, acquiring wealth, looked down snobbishly on all the foreignborn. Others prided themselves on pretentious houses and showy apparel and despised those who lived simply. Many held narrow views as to what was socially acceptable, and were intolerant of any who would think or act independently. An individualist from the first, Willa found this atmosphere stifling. In *The Song of the Lark*, her young musical artist, Thea, knows this; she must get away from just such a hostile environment.

AN INDEPENDENT SPIRIT

While at Red Cloud, however, Willa refused to be regimented. Fond of her family, she still jealously guarded her privacy. Her friends were people of wide-ranging interests - the Miners, who loved music; "Uncle Billy" Ducker, the English-born merchant who taught her the *Aeneid;* the cosmopolitan Mrs. Weiner, who introduced her to French novels; and several local doctors, who talked over science with her. She wore her hair shorter than was fashionable, and built herself a summer sleeping tent on the upper front porch. Her first ambition was to be a surgeon, and her Commencement address was a ringing defense of vivisection.

At the fledgling State University, in Lincoln, she fortunately encountered several stimulating professors who encouraged her to write: On one she based the character of Gaston Cleric, Jim's teacher in *My Antonia*. To help pay her way, she wrote for the local paper criticisms of dramas presented by acting companies on tour. Her reviews were lively and often caustic; these plus other experimental efforts proved to be good practice.

THE YEARS AT MCCLURE'S

In 1896, one year after her graduation, she accepted an editorial post in Pittsburgh. This was a large city with many cultural opportunities, of which she took full advantage. Then, after a decade divided between journalism and high-school teaching, she went to New York to join the staff of *McClure's Magazine*. Later she served as its managing editor. This noteworthy publication brought out works of such outstanding writers as Robert Louis Stevenson, Rudyard Kipling, and Stephen Crane. S.

S. McClure, its dynamic "idea man," had been a poor Irish farm boy raised in the Midwest. He was one more example for Miss Cather of what could be accomplished by native ability and unstinting effort.

By 1912 she had left McClure's to devote full time to her writing. In that year appeared her first novel, *Alexander's Bridge*. In it a middle-aged engineer, seemingly a devoted husband, seeks his lost youth in the love of an admiring actress. His failure to act decisively in this and other matters leads to his death when a new bridge of his collapses. Carefully planned and written with skill, the book showed psychological insight. It imitated somewhat the style of Henry James, whose works she regarded highly. Later she herself thought the novel unsatisfactory because she did not know its people well enough.

PIONEERS AND ARTISTS

From college days on she had used some of her experiences in Nebraska in short stories. Her decision to employ them in her later novels was due in part to advice given her by Isabelle Jewett. This perceptive New England writer urged her most strongly to re-create those scenes with which she was completely familiar.

O Pioneers!, the first of the prairie novels, appeared in 1913. Its dauntless heroine, Alexandra Bergson, is a Swedish immigrant girl whose vision and sustained effort at length bring rich returns from the farm land she has loved. *My Antonia*, published five years later, has a somewhat similar theme. Antonia Shimerda, a generous, good-hearted Bohemian girl, suffers many hardships after her father's suicide. Eventually, however, she becomes a happy wife and mother and enjoys prosperity on the farm she gave so much of herself to cultivate. This book was freer in form and used symbolism with greater artistry.

Between these two novels Miss Cather brought out *The Song of the Lark* in 1915. This long novel, more lavish in detail than the rest, describes the struggles of another type of creative personality to achieve a high goal. With the help of far-seeing friends and her own persistent efforts, Thea Kronborg escapes from the narrow confines of Moonstone and becomes a great opera star. The heroine reminds one at times of Miss Cather herself, but her story was also largely that of Olive Fremstad, a Swedish-born singer whose ascent to fame the author found remarkable.

POST-WAR PESSIMISM

Although disheartened by the increasing materialism and cultural shallowness in America, Miss Cather was hopeful for a time that the spirit of selfless dedication revived by World War I might continue to animate our national life. By 1922, however, her world, it seemed, "broke in two," as she saw greed, vulgarity, and intolerance more strongly entrenched than ever. In *One of Ours*, which appeared in that year, the mother of the dead war hero is ruefully grateful that her Claude never came back to be disillusioned. In *A Lost Lady*, which came out in 1923, the widow of the great pioneer railroad builder surrenders everything to the mean, petty, grasping lawyer, typifying the contemptible new ruling class. Two years later there followed *The Professor's House*, in which the hard-won gains of the earnest middle-aged scholar and of the brilliant young scientist are poured out to satisfy the extravagant whims of those who create nothing. These novels thus have pessimistic overtones.

RESTORING THE BRIGHT VISION

Yet Miss Cather also suggests ways in which the idealist can keep his vision bright even amid destructive influences. First of all he is strengthened by those who themselves have lofty standards. Jim, the saddened lawyer of *My Antonia*, derives new inspiration from meeting his Bohemian friend after two decades and finding her, "in the full vigour of her personality, battered but not diminished." Godfrey St. Peter, in *The Professor's House*, is able to put new heart into his work after he meets eager, high-minded Tom Outland.

Miss Cather further indicates that closeness to Nature can be helpful. Alexandra and Antonia live in satisfying harmony with their vast prairie country. Thea Kronborg and Tom Outland, like the author herself, found their lives enriched by sojourns in America's starkly beautiful Southwest. Its awesome canyons and mesas restored those dismayed by the small-mindedness in contemporary life. Its well-preserved cliff-dwellings of ancient tribes offered striking proof from the past of what even primitive man could achieve. Finally, there were traces everywhere of the good work of valiant early missionaries.

The novelist also undoubtedly believed that flagging idealism could be newly roused by steeping oneself in the heroism of earlier ages. In *Death Comes for the Archbishop* (1927), which many consider her masterpiece, she relates in fictional terms the story of two brave, selfless 19th-century French priests who give up the comforts of life at home to bring the finest elements of European civilization to New Mexico. For *Shadows on the Rock* (1931), she went back two hundred years further to the French settlement of Quebec. There, too, she found gallant pioneers enduring a rigorous climate, yet carrying on the best of their cultural traditions.

OTHER WORKS

Although these are her major works, Willa Cather wrote three other novels. *My Mortal Enemy* (1926) is a short one about a woman who eventually regrets having given up all for love. *Lucy Gayheart* (1935) is a poignant love story in which a high-spirited girl comes to accept the loss of her beloved just before her own untimely death. *Sapphira and the Slave Girl* (1940), in which the author drew upon her early memories of Virginia, tells of a jealous wife who unjustly suspects an attractive young servant. Miss Cather also published several collections of short stories, one volume of poems, and two books of essays. From the early days at McClure's to her death in 1947, Willa Cather made her home in New York, but enjoyed trips to Nebraska and the Southwest, France and Canada. She wrote much at her summer place off the coast of New Brunswick and in the quiet town of Jaffrey, New Hampshire, where she was eventually buried. She never married despite opportunities, possibly because she was too deeply absorbed in her work. She kept in close touch with her family, however, and maintained many rewarding friendships, especially with those in literary and musical fields.

AWARDS AND ATTACKS

For her contribution to American fiction, she received honorary degrees and other awards, including the Pulitzer Prize for *One of Ours*. Throughout her career she won the praise of almost all discriminating critics and still retains a high reputation. Yet not all aspects of her work have been universally commended. Some early commentators, for instance, asserted, and she later concurred, that the final sections of *The Song of the Lark* were inferior to the chapters on Moonstone. Others took issue with her account of the war in *One of Ours*. Still others have been critical of her seeming inability to handle effectively the love relationship between a man and a woman. Her over-all concern with the past and her frequently nostalgic tone has also been subject to discussion. Lionel Trilling has suggested that her regard for earlier ages indicates a "devitalization of spirit" stemming from an excessive sense of being personally isolated. Maxwell Geismar sees in this a kind of escapism, or running away from the life of her times. A recent critic, John H. Randall, believes that she glorified childhood too much at the expense of maturity.

LASTING CONTRIBUTIONS

Yet such criticism, valid or otherwise, do not take much away from what Francis X. Connolly has called her "immense and imperishable" contribution to our literature. For one thing she broadened the scope of American fiction. Her accounts of pioneer farming in Nebraska and of the adventures of missionaries in the Southwest were essentially without precedent.

Secondly, she developed with great artistry a characteristic style at once simple, polished, and precise. For her superb descriptive passages, she selected details carefully. She disliked undisciplined, wordy writing that strained to reveal all things about everybody. Her ideal was the novel that was "demeuble," or "unfurnished," except for what was truly essential. "The higher processes of art," she declared, "are all processes of simplification." The genuine realist was one who perceived all that was basic in a situation and conveyed this to the reader. Not everything had to be lengthily explained. A careful writer like Miss Cather could leave much to the mature reader's imagination, and her skillful use of symbols added richness without clutter.

Thirdly, she created memorable characters whose moral victories are hard won and whose rugged goodness has nothing in common with the weak, cloying kind exploited by sentimental fiction. Ernest Hemingway once described courage as "grace under pressure." Long after reading the Cather novels, many recall with pleasure heartening examples of this type of admirable behavior. They remember her rugged old Bishop Laval, ringing his Mass bell at 4 a.m., and her dying Ray Kennedy, gallantly considerate to the last. They think of Antonia soberly facing up to the bitter facts of her betrayal and of young Niel quietly postponing his studies for a whole year to help his beleaguered friends, the Forresters. They relive, too, moments of high exaltation - Alexandra's vision of flourishing farmlands, Thea singing gloriously amid the friendly Mexicans, Tom Outland experiencing for the first time alone the splendors of the mesa by night. In accepting the Nobel Prize for literature in 1949, William Faulkner asserted his belief that man was certain not only to survive but to prevail because he possessed "a spirit capable of compassion and sacrifice and endurance." Willa Cather's best work continues to have wide appeal because she too reveals this faith in humanity and because the stories she tells strengthen our confidence that men of the present and future can match, and perhaps even better, the shining record of the past.

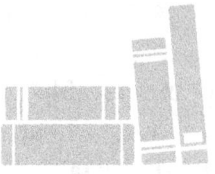

MY ANTONIA

INTRODUCTION

During a hot summer's train ride through Iowa, the narrator (conceivably Willa Cather herself) meets a childhood friend, Jim Burden. Now a successful New York lawyer, Burden is married to a brisk, insensitive woman of means, who fancies herself a patron of the arts. She seems incapable of enthusiasm, and the narrator dislikes her. Jim, however, is still the romantic personality he was as a boy.

On the trip, the two friends recall Antonia, a Bohemian girl they once knew who symbolize to both all that was fine and memorable in the Nebraska youth that they shared. Jim announces that he has been setting down all that he remembers about her. Months later, he brings his manuscript to the narrator's apartment, apologizing for its unrevised state and seeming lack of form. Deciding to add a title, he calls his piece *My Antonia*.

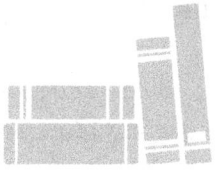

MY ANTONIA

TEXTUAL ANALYSIS

BOOK I: THE SHIMERDAS - CHAPTERS 1-8

Orphaned at ten, Jim makes the long train journey from his Virginia birthplace to his grandparents' farm in Nebraska. With him is Jake, a young farmhand. An amiable conductor tells him of an immigrant family in the next car. One daughter is a bright, pretty, brown-eyed girl who talks some English. Jim, however, is too shy to meet her. Arriving in Black Hawk by night, he sees the foreign group huddled amid their possessions. He himself is met by Otto, a wild-looking but kindly hired man, who drives him through the blackness to the farm.

Grandmother Burden, a lean, vigorous woman in her fifties, stands for "due order and decorum." Her white-washed kitchen is warm, clean, and inviting. Grandfather, bald but with a fine white curly beard, is reserved but gracious, and reads the Psalms beautifully.

Exploring his new terrain, Jim admires the flourishing farm but is most impressed with the unending miles of tall wine-red grass waving in the wind. Surrounded by it, he feels absorbed into something great and complete. This, he later decides, is what happiness is.

The Burdens visit the Bohemian settlers and find that their grasping countryman, Peter Krajiek, has sold them poor land and a wretched cave-like shelter. The family consists of the mother, a whining, inefficient housekeeper; 19-year-old Ambrosch, husky but sharp and wary; a small blonde girl, Yulka; a big, abnormal boy, Marek; and dark-haired 14-year-old Antonia, with large eyes and glowing skin. Gentle Mr. Shimerda, tall and slim, is a skilled weaver, who used to play the violin at weddings.

Living conditions are hard for the Shimerdas, but Jim and Antonia become fast friends as he teaches her English. He also admires her father, who seems sad and lonely. Jim rides over to see her on his pony. One chilly late fall afternoon, Antonia nurses back to life a dying insect. Its cracked voice reminds her of Old Hata, a storyteller in Bohemia. On another occasion, Jim, although terrified, kills a huge rattlesnake, and Antonia extols him to everyone.

They make friends with Pavel and Peter, two lonesome Russian settlers. Peter shares with them his precious melons. Pavel later becomes mortally ill and gasps out a tragic tale that both horrifies and fascinates the children. He and Peter once drove a sled with a bridal couple across dark, snowy Russian country. Attacked by hordes of ravenous wolves, occupants of other sleds died. Pavel sacrificed the bride and groom, and the two got back safely but were forced into exile. Since then ill luck has always haunted them. Pavel dies, and Peter leaves town after all that he owns is claimed by an unscrupulous money-lender.

CHARACTER ANALYSIS: THROUGH CHAPTER 8

Jim Burden

In this section Jim is encountered first as a man, then as a small boy. The older Jim is described as a success in his professional life and a failure in domestic matters. He has done well as counsel for a western railroad because of his intense love of the land and his vision. His married life has proved disappointing, however, because his wife has no wish to share his enthusiasms and finds his taste for simpler pleasures merely irritating. Although disillusioned, Jim is still boyishly romantic.

At ten, Jim combines shyness with a certain love of adventure. On the train he cannot bring himself to go up to meet the foreign girl, as the conductor suggests. Yet he enjoys reading about Jesse James and cannot wait to hear how the ferocious-looking Otto lost part of an ear. Going up with his grandmother to a remote potato patch, he remains alone after she leaves, despite warnings of possible rattlers. At this time he also reveals a sensitive, vaguely spiritual nature. Traveling over the dark roads to the farm, he feels as though he were canceled out of existence. Again, seeing the windblown seas of Nebraska grass, he has the sensation of being absorbed into something great and good.

In the developing friendship between him and Antonia, the girl takes the initiative. She is, of course, four years older, but he comes to resent her rather superior airs. He is therefore much relieved when his victory over the great snake gives him a certain preeminence. Recalling the snake episode as an adult, Jim amusedly plays down the heroism of his youthful feat. After all, the snake was fat and lazy, and the frightened boy struck from instinct rather than deliberate valor. He also notes sardonically the readiness with which the young champion accepted Antonia's glowing description of his bravery. He thus makes the boy seem self-centered, pompous, and somewhat lacking in humor.

Like his grandparents, also Virginia-born, Jim is reserved. He is embarrassed by the impulsive generosity of Antonia and her father. When he teaches the girl some English, she offers him a silver ring. Later her father promises to leave him a valuable Old World gun. Jim feels merely uncomfortable.

Yet he shares a sensitivity to beauty with the Shimerda pair. With Antonia he enjoys discovering the wonders of the Nebraska countryside, and he does not laugh when she and her father try to revive the frail, dying insect and talk sadly of the old storyteller whom children loved.

Antonia Shimerda

From the start, Antonia is pictured as bright, energetic, and vivacious. She is the first in her family to learn English. Obviously the favorite of her gentle, sensitive father, she is eager to learn and grateful for any help. She is strong, healthy, good-looking, and full of life.

She is also warm-hearted and generous. She offers her ring to Jim for teaching her English. Later when Jim kills the snake, she tells everyone how heroic he was. Uniformly affectionate toward her father, she even has some feeling for the weakest and frailest of creatures, as can be seen in the incident of the dying insect.

Finally, there is indication here that Antonia will be a forceful personality. She makes the initial move in the friendship with Jim, and he notes that as her English improves she expresses opinions on everything. It is at her suggestion that Jim and she stop off to see the holes of the prairie dogs, whereupon the big snake is disturbed and coils to strike. Moreover, Jim's very annoyance at her domineering manner indicates that the immigrant girl is not lacking in spirit.

Grandmother Burden

This Virginia-bred farm woman is strong, intelligent, hard-working, and kindly. When Jim first sees her on the morning after his arrival, she has been crying, doubtless because the boy's father, her son, is dead. Yet she is not one to let emotions get out of control. So she briskly invites Jim down to breakfast.

She runs a good, clean, orderly home. Her bright kitchen, with its geraniums and white curtains, and sweet-smelling gingerbread, speaks well for her sense of "due order and decorum." She is also good to her immigrant neighbors, bringing them provisions to help them get started. She is, however, repelled by effusive expressions of thanks and will find it hard to understand why a woman like Mrs. Shimerda cannot run a house more efficiently. Although she tries to make allowances, she cannot grasp fully the problems of those suddenly faced with the new customs and conditions of a totally strange land.

Grandfather Burden

In this section he is seen mainly as a dignified, industrious older man, whose white beard gives him the appearance of a patriarch from the Bible. Hardly the talkative type, he yet seems very much the head of the house. He runs his farm well and is deeply religious.

Mr. Shimerda

Always very careful of his attire, the tall, slim Mr. Shimerda is always the gentleman, just as his wife and Ambrosch are emphatically peasants. He is fond of Antonia and most insistent that she go on learning. He takes a kindly interest in Jim and sees in the Burdens a family who may help his daughter acquire the knowledge she needs.

He suffers much because of the miserable conditions in the cave and misses his homeland greatly. Except for shared moments with the more sanguine Jim and Antonia, he is a sad, lonely, isolated figure. For a time his spirits are raised when he strikes up a friendship with Peter and Pavel, whose Russian speech he can understand. When, however, Pavel dies and Peter leaves, he is more deeply disheartened than ever.

Comment: Through Chapter 8

The brief Introduction by the author seems at first unnecessary. Jim Burden's story of Antonia is complete in itself. Nevertheless, Willa Cather within its few pages establishes certain basic lines of development.

First of all, with a few vivid descriptive phrases she establishes the importance of the natural setting. A very real part in her story will be played by the prairie country itself. By referring to "never-ending miles of ripe wheat," the ever-present red dust, the "burning wind" and the "blustery winters," she suggests those "stimulating extremes" in her novel.

Secondly, through the comments of the narrator and Jim she indicates that unlike certain other writers of her time, such as Hamlin Garland and Frank Norris, she is not going to draw a bleak, pessimistic picture of life on mid-western farms. The two friends talk of a country "green and billowy beneath a brilliant sky" and allude to the "whole adventure" of their childhood.

Thirdly, the author, by her incidental remarks about Jim's wife, makes it clear that Jim did not grown up to marry Antonia. The Bohemian girl, from the first, is not the conventional heroine of a conventional love story, even though Jim has found her unforgettable. She is intended rather to symbolize "the country, the conditions," the great adventure of growing up in rural Nebraska during the 1880s.

We are in fact to consider Antonia virtually a new type of **epic** figure. The earlier **epic** heroes, like Achilles and Aeneas, were outstanding individuals who summed up the best traits of their respective cultures. Antonia, as we shall see, is no great warrior or world leader. Yet she does, in Miss Cather's view, embody the most admirable qualities of our western immigrant pioneers.

Finally, the Introduction tells us something about the form and style of the novel. In 1918, when *My Antonia* appeared, readers were accustomed to stories with tightly constructed, often predictable plots. Miss Cather, however, was attempting something new and different. She thus has Jim say that he has written down all that he remembers about his Bohemian friend without reorganizing or revising his material. Actually, the work has been carefully planned and written by Miss Cather to develop for us gradually a well-integrated portrayal of a character and a way of life. Yet she will do this by letting Jim recall key **episodes** seemingly at random rather than by using the standard devices of more conventional fiction.

Incidentally, the heroine's name, Antonia, is spelled in many editions and critical works with an accent over the first letter. Because of certain printing requirements the accent will be omitted in this book. The name should be pronounced with the stress upon the first syllable (AN-ton-ee-ah). Jim also refers to her sometimes as Tony. When there is actual dialog, Antonia's English is poor at first. Later it improves, but she never speaks with the fluency of her friend Lena Lingard, another immigrant girl.

In general, *My Antonia* is a work that draws heavily upon Willa Cather's own childhood experiences. She, too, left a Virginia birthplace to join grandparents on a Nebraska farm when she was about nine years old. Thus, many of the recollections of "Jim Burden" are based upon her own memories. Recent critical studies, notably *The World of Willa Cather*, by Mildred Bennett, have identified those Nebraska friends and relatives who were the originals for certain characters. The elder Burdens, for instance, resemble her grandfather and grandmother, William and Caroline Cather (Bennett, 10-11). Antonia's family, the Shimerdas, were drawn from the immigrant Sadileks she knew in her girlhood (Bennett, 46-51). The town of Black Hawk was Red Cloud, Nebraska, as she saw it in the 1880s.

The early chapters contrast sharply the living conditions of two groups of Nebraska settlers. The Burdens represent the well-established nativeborn farmers. Capable and industrious, they have built up a flourishing homestead. Their white wooden house is warm, clean, and comfortable. They also have a windmill and barns, granaries, pig-yards, and corncribs. Grandfather works well with the hired men, and Grandmother tends her vegetable garden and presides over a neat, well-run house. The newly arrived Shimerdas, on the other hand, have poor land and the worst of accommodations. They have few provisions, poor equipment, and not much capital. In addition, they do not know the language and must rely upon Krajiek, the unscrupulous fellow-countryman who has already cheated them shamefully. Jim and Antonia arrive in Nebraska together, but it is clear at once that the immigrant girl will have a much harder struggle. Yet if she does persevere and does overcome the formidable obstacles facing her, she may well prove the more remarkable character.

As in *O Pioneers!*, her earlier novel, Willa Cather will show her American readers a strong immigrant woman enduring much and eventually contributing a great deal to her adopted country. Yet the author is not a sentimentalist suggesting that all foreign settlers are good and all native-born settlers mean or weak. Here, whereas the Burdens are friendly and try to help the newcomers, the Shimerdas are cruelly exploited by another immigrant. Moreover, even within the family group, Mrs. Shimerda is greedy and ill-natured, young Ambrosch is sly, and Marek is hardly normal. Mr. Shimerda admittedly is charming, but mournful and ineffectual. Antonia stands out as much among her own people as she will later in other circles.

If Willa Cather is not crudely lauding all immigrants at the expense of all those born in America, neither is she indiscriminately favoring one culture rather than another. In these early chapters, a favorable portrayal is developed of Grandmother Burden, the Virginia-born standard bearer for "due order and decorum." She is a strong, able, good-hearted woman, and her orderly pleasant home is a civilizing force on the frontier. Antonia's mother is a European peasant. Physically she is sturdy. There is a toughness in her constitution that will enable her to survive rigors that will daunt her more refined, more sensitive husband. Mrs. Shimerda, Ambrosch, and Antonia all have enormous vitality. Yet Antonia's mother and brother also have the mean, grasping, small-minded natures of the peasant group at its worst. Their manners are rough, and they tend to be sly and sullen. More like her gracious father, Antonia, from the beginning, is shown to possess a warm, loving nature. As the story proceeds, however, she is subjected to two types of influence. Association with her mother and her brother has a coarsening effect. From her father, and later Mrs. Burden, she learns "nice ways." Miss Cather in this manner seems to hold up as ideal the combination of peasant vigor and determination and European or Southern American refinement, with its courtly generosity of spirit.

In this section much is made also of the emotional and imaginative response of Jim and Antonia to the natural beauty of the unspoiled land which both have suddenly come upon for the first time in their young lives. They come from vastly different backgrounds and are by no means possessed of identical personalities. Yet they do share a sensitivity to beauty, and they are both capable of enthusiasm. Miss Cather seems to approve highly of those who respond with feeling to whatever wonders they encounter. In the Introduction there is fondness suggested for the romantic Jim and none at all for his "unimpressionable" wife.

In her books Willa Cather, like such romantic poets as William Wordsworth, is much concerned with experiences that become important because some individual has felt strongly about them. The boundless prairie, with its gently blown red grass, is a fact that no Nebraskan can ignore. Yet there is no evidence that it proves inspiring to Mrs. Shimerda or Ambrosch.

Young Jim, however, is sensitive and imaginative. Alone out on the prairie, he responds to its vastness with his whole being. His enjoyment is unusually intense. He caught up in a kind of rapture. Antonia, too, is "impressionable" and responsive. As a result, their exploratory rambles through their new region, as well as their battle with the snake and their overhearing of Pavel's deathbed confession, all become part of the great adventure of growing up. Furthermore, such exciting **episodes** will provide them with precious memories which will enrich their subsequent lives.

The three most notable incidents in the second half of this section are the Old Hata **episode**, the killing of the snake, the Pavel's story of the wolves. Each is not only interesting in itself but revealing as to the richness and complexity of Willa Cather's art.

The dying insect is revived briefly by Antonia on a chill autumn afternoon. Here the author's use of striking contrasts is most effective, as she suggests a delicate balance between warmth and coldness, joy and sadness, life and death. On the one hand, there is the flowing sunshine with the lively rabbits darting about. The young people are enjoying their pleasant friendship, and Antonia herself seems to represent vitality and warmth. She coaxes the frail insect to sing again and even momentarily rouses some spark of animation in her disheartened father. She is making progress in learning to read English, and overjoyed that the rabbits her father has shot will mean "meat for eat, skin for hat."

At the same time, death is in the air. Winter is coming, and the day gradually darkens. Antonia tells Jim of badgers torn by dogs in the old country, and she recalls the aging storyteller, Old Hata. The insect, last of the small summer creatures, has been only "lured back to life by false pretenses"; and old Mr. Shimerda, although brightening up at the sight of Antonia, is actually failing fast. The interplay here of bright and dark **themes** is such as to raise a most insignificant occurrence to the level of a moving and memorable experience.

As for the snake battle, the incident reveals first of all how well Miss Cather can handle a good, exciting adventure tale. The description of the rattler's loathsome writhing and the boy's sick horror is vivid, and the ensuing action is blood-curdling enough. Then the pace changes, and the author shifts to comedy, almost in the manner of Mark Twain, as Jim Burden preens himself over is heroic feat. Finally, through the rueful comments of the adult Jim, she makes us see the very slight basis for so much self-congratulations.

Actually, although she has Jim, as a man, snort skeptically at dragon slayers in general, Miss Cather is not really cynical about all heroines. Her Antonia, for instance, seems at times an **epic** figure. Yet her conception of the heroic emphasizes not the big, showy act in which chance may play a major part, but rather a life of courageous endurance, accepting and overcoming hardships over the years.

The third account, that of the wedding party pursued by wolves, proves that the author can do ample justice to a stark horror piece. In a sense the short narrative is independent of the main plot. It is just a story that Antonia and Jim hear. Yet the author uses it skillfully. There is contrast, for instance, between the terrible agony of the dying Pavel and the fascinated interest of the two healthy, high-spirited young people. They are not inhuman. They can be sorry for a sick, suffering man, but they still find it wonderful to be in on something so fantastic and so shocking. Knowing this weird secret is one more bond between them, one more exciting moment in their great adventure.

In addition, there is the suggestion, not infrequent in Miss Cather's works, of the operation of fate or some sort of mysterious doom. She has had Jim previously feel an awareness of the power of Destiny as he was carried through the black night to his grandparents' farm. Now, in this story, there is no indication that Peter had much to do with the death of the unfortunate bride and groom Yet, having been with Pavel at the time, he has been continually the victim of misfortune. He is pictured as a hard-working, inoffensive man, anxious to please, but he seems forever doomed to meet with ill-luck.

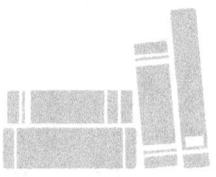

MY ANTONIA

TEXTUAL ANALYSIS

BOOK I: THE SHIMERDAS - CHAPTERS 9-15

After the first December snowfall, Jim takes Antonia and Yulka for a ride in his new sleigh, made for him by Otto, once a cabinetmaker's apprentice. The young people find the drive through the dazzling white scenery exhilarating although the girls shiver in thin dress and shawls.

The Burden home is warm and comfortable, and Grandmother sees to it that they have plenty of chicken and ham, pies, cakes, and puddings. The hired men labor hard and cheerfully, although neither will ever be rich. One night Otto tells an amusing story about his coming to America. He was asked then to look after the expectant wife of a friend. En route the lady had twins, and poor Otto had his hands full.

Some weeks later, hearing that the Shimerdas are in distress, the Burdens bring them provisions. Mrs. Shimerda embarrasses Grandmother with her tirades and tears. Antonia is more gracious, and Mr. Shimerda explains sadly that they left Bohemia with adequate funds but lost out through ruinous exchange rates and Krajiek's greed. As they leave, Mrs. Shimerda gives them a cupful of dried food, which she obviously treasures. Suspicious of anything so foreign, Mrs. Burden throws the flakes into the fire. Jim tastes one, however, and later learns that they were dried mushrooms brought from Europe.

At Christmastime, Jim makes a picture book for the Shimerda girls. Jake cuts down a small cedar, which the family trims with gingerbread, popcorn, and candles. Otto adds beautiful paper figures from Austria. On the day itself, Grandfather reads the Bible story and they breakfast on waffles and sausage. Later in the day Mr. Shimerda comes to call. He relaxes amid the civilized comforts of the Burden home and obviously returns with regret to his own cheerless hovel and self-pitying wife.

During the subsequent thaw, Mrs. Shimerda comes over with Antonia. The Bohemian woman whines enviously and seizes an iron pot. Jim is angry and reacts coldly when Antonia tells him that her father is ill and unhappy. She adds that it was her mother who insisted that they come to America to provide better opportunities for the children. Jim remains hostile, and the girl asks why his wealthy grandfather hasn't helped them with needed loans. Ambrosch, she declares, would surely pay him back.

On January 22, the Burdens learn that Mr. Shimerda has shot himself. Although the ground is frozen and travel is hard, Jim's family sends Otto for the coroner and the priest. Mrs. Burden goes over to comfort the women. Jim, alone at home, feels that Mr. Shimerda's unhappy spirit may linger in the burden home before starting back to Bohemia. Otto cannot reach the missionary priest, but Anton Jelinek, a strong and likable young Bohemian, arrives to help. He explains to Grandfather how much having a priest means to Catholics and impresses Mr. Burden with his "manly" faith.

Otto makes a coffin. Mr. Shimerda's frozen body is then buried, after some brief prayers by Grandfather, near the crossroads, in line with an old-country superstition about suicides. During the following months, Antonia gives up her studies and works hard with Ambrosch, becoming brown and husky, but losing her "nice ways." Jim and Jake have a brief feud with her brother, but Grandfather settles things amicably and hires her for kitchen work at harvesttime.

CHARACTER ANALYSIS: CHAPTERS 9-15

Jim Burden

In this section Jim's hot temper flares more than once. At age eleven he is not overly disposed to make allowances for those whom desperate circumstances drive to behave disagreeably. Acutely aware of all that the Burdens have done to aid the Shimerdas, he is furious when Antonia's mother snatches his grandmother's iron pot. If the Bohemians are in need, it is somehow their fault. If they could not manage more successfully, they should not have come to America at all. Jim thus as a boy has little sympathy for those who won't act politely toward their benefactors.

He is angered again after Mr. Shimerda's death when the surly Ambrosch seems uninterested in returning a borrowed harness and then throws one back in poor condition. After a scuffle in which Jake knocks the Bohemian youth down, as Antonia and her mother voice fiery protests, Jim decides that he never wants to see any of these foreigners again, including Antonia. He will change his mind, of course, but on several future occasions he will again prove a young man readily roused to indignation.

He is also, however, inclined to be generous when not offended by slights. He is delighted to offer Antonia and Yulka a ride in his new horse-drawn sleigh. He even gives his long comforter or scarf to the half-frozen younger sister, thereby leaving himself open to a quinsy attack. In addition, he expends much effort in putting together an attractive picture book as a Christmas present for the two immigrant girls.

Other traits, suggested in the first section, are again evident here. First of all, Jim relishes adventure or excitement. Having liked Mr. Shimerda, he is saddened by the old man's suicide. Yet the general hubbub, the coming and going of neighbors during the period following the tragedy, he finds almost pleasurable.

Secondly, he seems sensitive here as before to beauty of various types. He enjoys the bracing drive through the snowy countryside. He finds enchanting the Christmas tree with Otto's Austrian paper decorations. He is also moved by the stark simplicity of the burial service on the bleak hillside.

Thirdly, he again gives evidence of a vaguely mystical strain. He resolutely dismisses the Catholic view that the soul of Mr. Shimerda may suffer in Purgatory because of the old man's rash action. Instead he fancifully imagines the spirit of the sad, homesick Bohemian pausing in the comfortable warmth of the Burden kitchen, then winging its way back to Europe.

Antonia Shimerda

If Jim reveals a mettlesome personality in this section, so does Antonia. When Jim criticizes her family, she replies heatedly and suggests that the Burdens could have done more to help their neighbors financially. Again, when Jake strikes the surly Ambrosch, she irately declares that she will no longer be friends with Jim and the young farmhand.

After her father's death, which leaves her heartbroken, she becomes for a time much more like her peasant mother and Ambrosch. All three work strenuously to make the farm prosper. Antonia, sunburned and strong, does the rough chores of a man and takes pride in closely rivaling her brother. Seeing her during these months, Jim finds her less feminine, more coarse in manner. Yet, in general, Antonia throughout the book is going to be held up to admiration as a woman of strength and determination. Her resolute acceptance of farm responsibilities here prepares us for her later triumphs over disasters that would destroy a weaker individual.

In addition, Antonia is refreshingly level-headed. Despite her annoyance over the blow to Ambrosch, she comes promptly to Grandfather Burden when one of her horses seems close to death. Moreover, no false pride prevents her coming to work in Grandmother's kitchen. She is obviously delighted to be there, keeps up a cheerful clatter with the pans, and pleases everyone with her hearty good humor. In quieter moments she wistfully admits that she likes life at the Burdens. She would have the nicer, more feminine ways that Jim so admires, had she the advantages that have always been his.

Grandmother Burden

In this section, as before, Mrs. Burden is the ideal homemaker and good neighbor. She is especially thoughtful at the time of the Shimerda tragedy. She readily offers to go over to console the bereft women, and she urges Jake to take a good horse to ride for priest and coroner, even though the trip through the snow may overstrain the animal.

She also, on occasion, shows admirable firmness. At the funeral services when Mrs. Shimerda foolishly tries to make the terrified little Yulka bid her father good-bye, the older woman briskly and decisively intervenes.

Yet she also is shown to have a certain narrowness of outlook. She cannot see why Mrs. Shimerda, a stranger speaking little English, has not known enough to set up a hen house and keep her family supplied with eggs and poultry. She has small patience with the other woman's housekeeping methods and throws out the mushrooms. Moreover, when Mr. Shimerda kills himself, she is surprised that he could have been so inconsiderate. All in all, she never does seem to grasp very well the dire needs and problems of the uprooted Europeans.

Mr. Shimerda

When the Burdens bring over supplies, Mr. Shimerda is grateful but deeply distressed that his family must take charity. He is a man of dignity and pride, explaining almost pathetically to his benefactors that he had some position in the old country. During the Christmastime visit, he momentarily relaxes, and we catch a glimpse of the genial Continental man of books and music he was in less rigorous climes. His suicide soon afterwards evidences his deep despair, but even before dying he goes quietly off and folds his clothes neatly, fastidious to the end.

Mrs. Shimerda

Usually whining and disagreeable, Mrs. Shimerda shows here that she is also grasping and mean. She seizes Mrs. Burden's iron pot on the ground that her hostess has more than she has. Later she makes an absurd attempt to avoid making final payments on a cow sold to her by Grandfather.

She also seems at times not overly intelligent. She does not learn the new language or new customs easily. Her handling of the frightened Yulka at the funeral is not sensible, and her efforts to elude Mr. Burden and to repudiate her promise to pay for the cow are ludicrous.

On the other hand, she is sometimes oddly shrewd. When Jake strikes Ambrosch, she rides in to prefer charges. Moreover, after her husband's death, she encourages Antonia to compete with Ambrosch, thus spurring the girl on to greater efforts.

Although generally an unsympathetic character, she has some good points. Her insistence upon coming to America derived from her vision of a better life for her children. In addition, she is not wholly lacking in gratitude. In fact, her emotional displays of thankfulness sometimes prove more embarrassing than her rudeness. Thirdly, she does eventually prove a fair housekeeper. When Jim visits the Shimerdas in the spring, she serves him fresh bread on an oilcloth-covered table.

Finally, although superstitious about the burial of suicides at crossroads, she is also genuinely pious, praying devoutly for the soul of her husband.

Grandfather Burden

The old patriarch has several roles to play in this section. For one thing, he is the community leader. At the time of the Shimerda tragedy, all those concerned come to his house and look to him for direction. When, for instance, Jake and the coroner suggest that Mr. Shimerda was actually murdered by Krajiek, Grandfather proves the theory untenable and establishes the fact of suicide.

Secondly, Grandfather is the peacemaker. When Jake and Jim come back furious after the fight with Ambrosch, he refuses to take the fracas seriously. He goes on helping Ambrosch to purchase the best farm animals for his needs, and he readily assists Antonia with the sick horse. Afterwards, he generously waives the final payments on the cow, and helps the brother and sister earn necessary cash by hiring both for the summer harvesting.

Thirdly, he is the man of faith, positive as regards his own religious convictions, yet capable of respecting the beliefs of others. When the Catholic Mr. Shimerda makes the Sign of the Cross while kneeling before the Christmas tree, Grandmother fears that her husband will protest. Grandfather remains silent, however, remarking quietly later, "The prayers of all good people are good." Subsequently, he argues with Anton Jelinek regarding the necessity of prayers for the dead. Yet he speaks admiringly of the young Bohemian's serious concern about such matters and treats him with grave courtesy. Then, on the day of the funeral, at the widow's request, he prays aloud for those left behind and entrusts the soul of the deceased to God's mercy.

Ambrosch Shimerda

Ambrosch appears surly and disagreeable, if not irresponsible, when he misuses the borrowed harness and is rude about it to Jake. He is not, however, lazy. He is willing to take over farm burdens and to work hard. He is also strongly religious. Jim is surprised how fervently he prays for his father. Later, although he has not much money, he uses Marek's wages for Masses for Mr. Shimerda's soul.

Comment: Chapters 9-15

There is some discussion among critics as to whether this novel is essentially the story of Antonia or of both the Bohemian girl and Jim Burden. Even the title is open to more than one interpretation. What does the my mean in *My Antonia*? Does it mean merely that the narrator can tell us only what he knows about her? Even as a boy he is out of touch with her for considerable periods, and in later life he will make his home far from her Nebraska farm country. Or does the my mean that the heroine described for us is the Antonia who serves as one of the major factors in Jim's progress toward maturity? In other words is she important primarily as an interesting individual or as one of Jim's treasured memories?

Either way, the events described in this section of the work crucially affect the relationship. Hitherto, despite the economic handicaps of the Shimerdas, Jim and Antonia have been carefree young people happily exploring the countryside. The suicide of the girl's father abruptly alters everything. She was learning English quickly and might have gone on to school with Jim. And present to guide her would have been her cultivated father, who was fond of books, music, and good talk. Instead, she will have no time for further studies. She must take on the most arduous of farm chores and do the work of a man. "Things will be easy for you," she tells Jim. "But they will be hard for us." She will go on to work as a hired girl and eventually wed a poor immigrant. He will go through the university and travel much abroad. At the very end of the story Jim will talk of those "early accidents of fortune which predetermined" their lives. The great fact that sets Antonia's life course is the violent death of her beloved father.

This section also develops further the idyllic, or extremely favorable, picture of life on the Burden farm. Peace and plenty, good order, and an over-all spirit of kindliness are everywhere apparent. Outside the cold winter winds may howl. Inside there can be found warmth, enough food for a feast, and happy, evenings with popcorn and taffy, song fests and story telling. As a novel, *My Antonia* is much concerned with life within the home. Within its pages three highly satisfactory households will be described. This is the first, the Burden home. The second will be that of the Harlings in Black Hawk; the third, in the final chapters, that of Antonia herself. In each instance an ideal is held up for our admiration, and the scene is described with an almost lyric enthusiasm that enhances its appeal.

By way of contrast we are also given glimpses of households far from pleasant. First, we have the Shimerda cave, dark and dismal, with a complaining, ineffectual woman doing little to make conditions better. Later we will see something of the nightmare home life of the moneylender Wick Cutter, and we have already heard of Jim's unsatisfactory domestic life with his handsome, coldhearted wife.

One other aspect is worth noting. In these chapters much is made of the hard work and generosity of the hired men, Jake and Otto. Together they provided Jim with his delightful Christmas tree. Yet they are, and will always be, rootless men. They are regarded with pity because they will never know the solid joys of those who have homes and families of their own and can build toward a brighter future.

If, however, this is a section singing the praises of domesticity, it also provides varied examples of prejudices that can make relations between groups more difficult. One of the most revealing occurs at the time of Mr. Shimerda's death. Inasmuch as the ground is frozen and travel is extremely difficult, funeral arrangements cannot easily be made. A request is thus made to the Norwegians, who have a cemetery nearby, to let the grave be dug on their land. They refuse, whereupon Grandmother is incensed against such "clannish" foreigners. Prejudice is also shown when Jake, infuriated by Ambrosch, decides that all foreigners are the same and cannot be trusted. At that time, Jim, too, declares hotly that all are like "Krajiek and Ambrosch." On the other hand, a decent, good-hearted young man like Anton Jelinek helps to improve the community status of his people; and Grandfather, through his wise and tolerant pronouncements, also helps to end feuds and encourage friendlier attitudes. He even saves the worthless Krajiek from being charged with the one crime of which he is not guilty.

As regards the artistry of Willa Cather in handling this material, we see again how subtly she has linked the changing seasons with the events described. It is obvious, of course, that the rigors of the Nebraska winter serve to deepen Mr. Shimerda's despair and thus precipitate his suicide. Yet the vivid descriptions here of the cold bleakness of the landscape intensify the starkness of the tragedy. This is the first crucial year of the great adventure. Jim and Antonia first joyously explored Nebraska when the tall red grass was blowing in the warm September wind. Then the chill set in, and the incidents described were more somber. These included the stories of the evil snake, the dying insect, and the ravenous wolves. Now, in this section, there is the grim, bitter cold. The Shimerdas suffer in their cheerless cave, and the father kills himself. Spring, however, brings hope, and the Bohemians begin to make progress. Then by the time of the summer harvest, misunderstandings end, and Antonia and Jim are happily reunited at the Burdens. Antonia, high-spirited and healthy, enjoys getting vegetables from the garden in the morning sunshine. She and Jim admire together the wonders of a magnificent electric storm that sends thunder crashing around them one close, hot night.

If the nature descriptions are thus used skillfully to highlight successive incidents, we also find the same effective use of contrast that was evident in the earlier chapters. The most striking example of this is the Christmas scene at the Burdens. Here there is everything to make a young boy pleased with his new home. The tree, with Otto's paper ornaments, is splendid, and everyone seems eager to do his part to make the holiday festive. The visit of Mr. Shimerda, however, makes all aware of the misery of the immigrant group. For a few brief hours, this cultivated European gentleman seems to relax and almost cheer up. Yet the Burdens know, as he does, that as night falls he must return to the dark, wretched cave. Joy and sadness, warmth and cold are thus interwoven.

Other uses of contrast may also be recalled. Grandfather Burden is sensible and tolerant, as opposed to the hotheaded Jake and Jim. Anton Jelinek is the admirable young Bohemian, as against the mean disagreeable Ambrosch. The neighborly helpfulness of the Burdens and their friends is quite different from the lack of cooperation shown by the Norwegians who will not allow the burial in their cemetery.

It must again be pointed out that the Introduction spoke of the adventure that was shared by all who grew up together during the 1880s in Nebraska. The whole series of events connected with the Shimerda suicide would be likely to leave a deep impression on those closely affected by the tragedy. This Willa Cather would know well, for Francis Sadilek, the model for the fictional Mr. Shimerda, actually did commit suicide, too, and was buried near the crossroads as the novel indicates. Throughout the story the death of Antonia's father will be referred to quite frequently as Jim and the girl meet again at different stages of their lives. The burial scene on the hillside, a heartbreaking experience, is something shared, something deeply felt that will be impossible for either ever to obliterate from his memory.

It was Willa Cather's belief that the most crucial years in an individual's development, those in which he was likely to store up his most vital impressions, were those between the ages of nine or ten and about fifteen.

My Antonia is particularly interesting because it is in effect a double illustration of what she meant. In terms of the fiction, Jim as a man and later Antonia as a woman will refer to the shared experiences of their early years as the most memorable of all. In fact, the Introduction indicates that Jim is not by any means merely jotting down a few casual recollections. He may apologize for the unrevised state of his manuscript, but he makes it quite clear that he is relating events that meant much to him not only at the time that they occurred but also during the years have passed since then.

In addition, we must keep in mind the strong autobiographical element in the work. Critics generally are convinced that a great many of the reactions and opinions attributed to Jim, are actually those of the author herself. She, too, discovered Nebraska as he did, rode around the countryside on her pony, enjoyed the company of her Virginia-born grandparents, and made many friends among the Bohemians and other groups of immigrant settlers. If her descriptions here are vivid and her scenes amazingly convincing, it seems probable that the experiences of her Nebraska girlhood, on which she drew so plentifully, did in fact leave on her a powerful permanent impression.

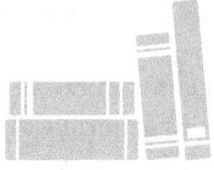

MY ANTONIA

TEXTUAL ANALYSIS

BOOK II: THE HIRED GIRLS - CHAPTERS 1-7

Three years after Jim's arrival in Nebraska, the Burdens rent their farm to the Widow Steavens and move into Black Hawk. There Jim can obtain further schooling. After settling the family in their new home near the edge of town, Otto heads back toward the wilder West, and Jake goes with him. Jim never sees either of these good men again.

Black Hawk is a pleasant clean little town with board sidewalks and white fences around grass plots. Jim misses the farm but likes his river view there. Because the Burden house is the first met upon entering town, country friends often stop there to leave their horses. Jim likes the company, but misses seeing Antonia. The widow Steavens says that Ambrosch is working her too hard. Grandmother hopes to get her work with their new neighbors, the Harlings.

The wife of a successful cattle merchant, Mrs. Harling was born in Norway, coming to America at age ten. A stocky, vigorous little woman, she has a fiery temper, but is also quick to laugh. She has strong feelings about everything. Her children include Charles, sixteen; the musically inclined Julia; the tomboyish Sally; and sensitive little Nina. The oldest girl, Frances, is chief clerk for her father. She knows all about credits, and her business acumen is widely respected. She works often with Grandfather Burden to save the farmers from the money-lender, Wick Cutter.

In August the Harlings lose their cook, and Grandfather recommends Antonia. Dealing with Ambrosch for the girl's services, the hearty Mrs. Harling is amused by his inept attempts to drive a hard bargain. She agrees to pay the girl three dollars a week.

Jim is jealous when Antonia obviously admires Charley Harling, baking nut cakes for him and doing his mending. In general, however, Jim has good times next door, especially when the lordly Mr. Harling is not home to demand quiet.

One evening a young blonde girl in blue, with a low, pleasant voice, arrives to visit Antonia. This is Lena Lingard, daughter of a poor Norwegian farmer, who has come to work for Mrs. Thomas, the local dressmaker. She tells them that another friend, Tiny Soderball, is set to work at the hotel, the Boys' Home. Mrs. Harling and Frances eye Lena with some suspicion, having heard stories already about her romances. Some were scandalized, for instance, when Ole Benson, married unhappily to "Crazy Mary," enjoyed talking to the gentle Lena in the fields. His wife, enraged, threatened the girl with a corn-knife. Lena denies that she did anything amiss. After this Jim sees Lena often in town, and at Christmas both help her little brother pick out presents for Mrs. Lingard.

After dreary nights on the farm, Antonia is happy at the Harlings. Evenings she contentedly sews nice clothes for herself.

She also tells stories. One grim one is of a tramp denied beer at a farm where he worked at harvest-time. Wild-eyed he dove into the threshing machine and died. Another time, Jim, Antonia, and Lena visit Tiny at the hotel, when her strict employer, Mrs. Gardner, has gone to Omaha to see Booth and Barrett in a play. The young people hear a visiting Negro pianist, Blind d'Arnault, give a rhythmically exciting impromptu concert. Jim and Antonia find it thrilling.

CHARACTER ANALYSIS: BOOK II, CHAPTERS 1-7

Jim Burden

At the time of the funeral of Mr. Shimerda, Jim was not insensitive to the sadder aspects of the situation, but he did like the company that kept coming to the Burden farm. This suggestion of the lonely boy who enjoys social gatherings is developed further in these chapters. First of all, Jim is pleased that the farmers coming into town stop for a time at his house. Nor does he mind running extra errands to get extra bread or steak for them. He also finds delightful the pleasant evenings at the Harlings. As winter comes on, the town often seems cold, bleak, and dreary. Yet he finds color and warmth at their home, and happily dives through the hedge to enjoy charades, a costume party, or even a dancing lesson. He likes to hear Mrs. Harling play selections from the operas, and he listens attentively to Antonia's stories.

He mentions in passing that he has quickly become used to school life, adding that he would be as wild as any of the other boys were it not for Mrs. Harling's restraining influence. There has been previous indication that Jim can be hot-tempered, but although he mentions more than once a tendency toward wildness, it is never particularly obvious in his actions. He will, it is true, court social disapproval by associating with the hired girls, who are considered by the town to be members of a lower class. Except for this, however, he is hardly the recklessly defiant type. There is also some suggestion that he is jealous of Charley, whom Antonia admires. This, too, seems far from serious.

Antonia Shimerda

Antonia loves life. From the first she is happy at the Harlings. Young and strong, she is eager to learn, willing to work, and delighted to be part of a big, busy, cheerful household. Cooking for such a sizable group would in those days require long hours of strenuous effort. Yet Antonia is so full of youthful energy and high spirits that she is always ready to run races or take part in hay fights with the children and make them extra cookies and taffy in the evening.

This vital young Bohemian girl is also by nature creative, with an artistic strain not surprising in a violinist's daughter. Here she is seen making slippers for herself and sewing pretty clothes. When Frances teaches them all to dance, Antonia proves the most likely pupil of all. Moreover, she is a good storyteller, as is evident from her chilling yarn about the tramp and the threshing machine. Finally, both she and Jim are much moved by the rhythmical playing of Blind d'Arnault, whom they hear that Saturday night at the Boys' Home.

She is not, however, as aggressive as some of her friends. She receives Lena Lingard with only limited cordiality because she fears that Mrs. Harling may be displeased if she welcomes someone who has been the subject of gossip. Again, when asked to dance by the salesmen listening to Blind d'Arnault, Antonia seems alarmed at first and looks to the others for reassurance.

Finally, she is kind and generous. Admiring Charley, she packs special lunches for his hunting trips, mends his ball-gloves, feeds his dog, and bakes his favorite nut cakes. For the others she makes candy and cookies, and she is always gentle with little Nina who so readily bursts into tears.

Grandmother Burden

With the move into town Mrs. Burden ceases to figure prominently in the story. She is described as busy with such community activities as church suppers and missionary society work, but Jim seems to spend most of his free time visiting the Harlings. She is, however, responsible for getting Antonia the post as cook. This good office, reveals first of all, her continuing neighborly concern. Ever since the girl lost her father, Mrs. Burden has wanted in some way to make Antonia's life a little easier.

Secondly, it indicates further how much she desires Antonia to have "nice ways." She remembers Mr. Shimerda as a "genteel old man" and shudders to think of his pretty daughter working out in the fields with rough threshers. Not one ordinarily given to asking favors, Grandmother anxiously entreats Mrs. Harling to try Antonia, for she knows that in such a pleasant environment the girl will learn much of value. For her part Antonia promises to be the kind of young woman that Grandmother will "like better," and within the month she is speaking English as well as any of the children. In later life, Antonia will tell Jim that were it not for her service at the Harlings, she might have brought up her own sons and daughters as "wild rabbits." So Mrs. Burden achieves her object.

Amusingly enough, Grandmother fears lest the disagreeable Ambrosch and his mother discourage Mrs. Harling from engaging Antonia by unreasonable demands. With this in mind, she shrewdly corners the sullen young man and suggests that it would improve his credit were his sister to work for the successful cattle dealer. Yet the younger, more vigorous, and less easily daunted Mrs. Harling sails in and good-naturedly bargains with the greedy Old World pair. She later laughingly confesses to Mrs. Burden that she is probably "more at home with that sort of bird." This is undoubtedly true. Remember how ill at ease, for all her neighborly intentions, Grandmother always was in the presence of the Shimerdas with their tears, tantrums, and extravagant expressions of gratitude? She is always a lady with a strong sense of decorum.

Mrs. Harling

Born in Norway, Mrs. Harling is stocky and vigorous, with bright, sparkling eyes and a rosy complexion. Notable for energy and enthusiasm, she is generally good natured, although she can, on occasion, reveal a fiery temper. Here she is seen as a capable homemaker, a good wife and mother. She is kind to Jim, the young boy from the next house, but will tolerate no wildness. If he causes little Nina to cry, he is sent home. She is also a good friend to Antonia, her young cook. The fact is that they are said to have much in common. Both are independent and emphatic about their preferences. Both are fond of children, animals, and music. Both are proud and generous, and both thoroughly enjoy life. Mrs. Harling's cheerful confidence in her ability to handle a situation is evident in her bargaining session with Ambrosch. It is also apparent that she is an enlightened employer for her time, since she pays fairly high wages and insists that the girl not be expected to turn back all that she earns to her brother. Finally, she is a reasonably shrewd judge of character. She likes Antonia from the first, is unimpressed by the ranting Ambrosch, and is decidedly skeptical about Lena Lingard's demure denials of frivolous leanings.

Frances Harling

The oldest and least carefree of the Harling children, Frances is intelligent and hardworking. since her brother Charley is destined for Annapolis, she has become her demanding father's business assistant. She has a good head for finance. She knows credits, as those thinking to outsmart her have learned to their sorrow. She is also, however, warm and generous. She not only saves hardpressed farmers from being cheated by the money-lender, Wick Cutter, she also takes a personal interest in their families, visiting them, attending their social functions, and sending gifts. Although her hours as clerk are long, she still finds time to teach Jim and the others dancing. She is gracious to Lena, with whose background she is thoroughly familiar, and quietly reassures the troubled Antonia that Lena as a visitor if she behaves herself.

Lena Lingard

A beautiful blonde girl, with a low, sweet voice, Lena is the daughter of a very poor farmer with many other children. She is sorry for her mother and happy to use her wages to assist her family. She is seen here helping her small brother choose Christmas presents. Nevertheless, she is determined never again to endure the hardships that she knew when herding her father's cattle. She has already stirred up gossip, and it is clear that she will be much admired by men. Yet, while she hopes to have a good time, she is delighted to be able to work with the local dressmaker. She likes fine fabrics and knows that she can handle them well. This means that she who formerly had only ragged clothes will be able to dress attractively. She is also ambitious and knows that by building a successful career for herself she can forever escape the farm drudgery she has come to loathe.

Comment: Book II, Chapters 1-7

In this section the autobiographical element is again worth noting. Willa Cather moved to Red Cloud, here known as Black Hawk, when she was eleven, in 1884, and lived there until 1890. The town when she came was about thirteen years old and numbered some 3,000 people. The houses, as mentioned, all had fences. These were to prevent stray flocks from destroying lawns.

The Harlings were the Miner family, who lived near the Cathers. Miss Cather actually dedicated *My Antonia* to two of the daughters, Carrie and Irene (Bennett, 93). Mrs. Miner, who served as model for Mrs. Harling, had died just at the time the novelist was planning the book. Her death revived many precious memories, and Miss Cather drew upon her recollections to draw an affectionate, true-to-life portrait of her old friend. Usually, like most writers of fiction, she created character by freely combining impressions of various people. Here, however, she wanted to represent Mrs. Miner as faithfully as possible (Bennett, 50-60).

Like the fictional Mrs. Harling, Mrs. Miner was Norwegian by birth. Her husband ran a general store in Red Cloud, and their daughter, Carrie, the model for Frances, served there as bookkeeper. Mary Miner suggested Julia, Margie was the tomboyish Sally, and their brother Hughie was Charley in the novel (Bennett, 44-46, 59-64). Incidentally, there was music in the Miner home, too, for the lady of the house was the daughter of an oboe soloist and had grown up to become a fairly accomplished pianist (Bennett, 59-60).

As for Antonia, the original Annie Pavelka did come to work at Mrs. Miner's. Willa Cather may have known her while the girl was still on the farm, but she became closely acquainted with her at this time. As in the book, the Bohemian family did try to claim her total wages, but Carrie Miner refused to yield. The popularity of the young servant with the children is also based on fact. Annie, too, made herself house slippers as described in the novel, and she was always willing to make Hughie's favorite nut cakes (Bennett, 48).

This section also reflects two of Willa Cather's major interests, drama and music. When the hired girls and Jim go up to the Boys' Home for the impromptu recital, they learn that Mrs. Gardner, the strong-minded woman who runs the hotel, has gone to Omaha to hear Booth and Barrett. When Willa Cather was a girl, she begged to be taken to hear Edwin Booth and Lawrence Barrett when they played in Omaha. The two famous actors, with their noteworthy Shakespearean troupe, went on tour in 1887. They played in 68 cities and towns throughout the United States. Later in Lincoln, Miss Cather worked as a drama critic. It may also be mentioned here that the Gardners, of the Boys' Home, resemble Mr. and Mrs. Holland, who ran the Holland House in Red Cloud (Bennett, 89-90).

Miss Cather also liked music, preferring, however, to hear and discuss it rather than to play it (Bennett, 153-4). Her enjoyment of the contributions of Negro entertainers is obvious here from her enthusiastic description of Blind d'Arnault. Although the portrait is a composite one, she said that she based it largely upon the life of a pianist of her day, Blind Boone (Bennett, 248). *My Antonia* was published in 1918. Today a writer might be less likely to talk in such general terms about Negroes. Miss Cather writes with admiration, but is her manner also somewhat condescending?

This section of the novel essentially is concerned with the move to town of the Burdens, Antonia, and the other hired girls. It is the ending of a way of life for them and the beginning of another. For one thing, it brings to a close the story of pioneer farming represented by the Burden household as described in the first section. When the boy Jim first came to Nebraska, his grandparents had already been there for some ten years. During that time they had subdued their portion of the wild prairie and built up a flourishing farm. Instead of the crude sod shelters of the newly arrived, they now had a warm and comfortable white frame house, as well as barns, granaries, and a windmill. They had hired help during the year and brought in extra workers at harvesttime. Their food supply was more than ample; they had plenty to share with the less fortunate.

When they move, all is changed. First of all, Jake and Otto leave, for they are no longer needed. Ordinarily this might not seem very significant. Farmhands often move from one place to another. Yet Miss Cather, through Jim, stresses repeatedly the idea that these two good, simple men, hard-working and kindly, are rootless types who will never have homes and families of their own. Attached to a solid, well-run menage like the Burdens', they acquire status in the community, and their lives somehow take on more meaning. When the poor, ignorant, hot-tempered Jake cuts down the tree for Jim or watches his language in the presence of Grandmother, he is not merely paid help. In a very real sense, he is one of the family. The same can be said of Austrian Otto when he tells his adventure yarns, provides the beautiful Christmas decorations, or puts together a coffin for Mr. Shimerda and leads the hymn singing at the funeral. With the breaking up of the farm, however, the pair head for the West, vaguely seeking adventure. After one post card from a mining camp, they are never heard from again. They have been set adrift, the book implies, to become two more restless wanderers.

Even the Burdens, however, seem to lose stature with the move. Grandfather is said to have become a church deacon. Whenever Frances Harling comes over to visit him, he is flattered, and the two work out ways of saving the farmers from the money-lender's clutches. Later Grandfather will let it be known to Anton Jelinek that he does not want Jim seen in the Bohemian's decent, respectable saloon. Both he and Grandmother are aging and might well be expected to become less active. Yet with the move into town, there is certainly a startling loss here of effectiveness as creative individuals. It is true that Mrs. Burden does make one more vital contribution by helping to free Antonia from the domination of Ambrosch. Nevertheless, it is also worth noting that she must now send her to the Harlings rather than bring her into her own home. To be sure, she will provide needed assistance during one more crisis in the girl's life, but she will also stop Jim from attending town dances patronized largely by hired help. In general, Grandmother ceases to be the forthright, energetic woman of the house and no longer dominates the domestic scene. Jim, for his part, dives through the hedge to the Harling's house.

There he finds the warmth, the companionship, and the social life that he craves. The move into town makes possible the further schooling that will enable him to go on to college and the university and build a successful career as a lawyer. Yet with the breaking up of the Burden farm household, he becomes, almost like Jake and Otto, a young man without a clearly established position in the family. At the Harlings, he is a welcome outsider, but still an outsider, and there is little to hold him in the town house of two retired old people. On the farm, he might gradually be taking over his inheritance, a junior partner in a going concern. As it is, he will flee to the East, as the hired men fled westward. And as we learned from the Introduction, he, too, will never really be able to establish a happy, productive home like that of the Burden farm.

As was mentioned before, three ideal homes are described in *My Antonia:* those of the Burdens as farmers, the Harlings, and Antonia in later life. In this section the Harling household is described. It is a well-run home, with many children, headed by an autocratic father and a strong-minded, lively, capable mother. The fact that both parents are such forceful, determined personalities might suggest the possibilities of conflict. Mrs. Harling, for instance, likes music and all the gaiety and excitement of home costume parties and dances. Mr. Harling, by contrast, likes a quiet house and demands the undivided attention of his wife. Yet a nice balance is maintained, because the lord and master is fortunately away frequently on business. In this way Miss Cather's independent and self-reliant Mrs. Harling can run things most of the time her way, and yet graciously indulge her husband's whims when he happens to be at home. Actually, when he does make an important, and rather harsh decision later concerning Antonia, Mrs. Harling, as the consistently dutiful wife, does not oppose him in any way. Yet having paid her respects in this way to traditional standards, Miss Cather still shows us her admirable homes as run by sturdy vital women. On the farm Grandfather was a man of few words and was usually out working with the hired hands. Only when the outside crisis of the Shimerda tragedy developed, did he begin to play an important role. We shall therefore not be surprised eventually to find that Antonia's husband is off attending a fair, when Jim after many years comes to call, or that he later proves to be far less decisive than the story's heroine. Incidentally, it may be noted that it is Mrs. Gardner, not her amiable Johnny, who runs the Boy's Home, that it was Mrs. Shimerda who insisted that the family come to America, and that even the assertive Ambrosch will at length be bossed by a fat wife. Miss Cather, in general, tends to draw iron-willed women. This is equally evident in others of her novels, such as *O Pioneers!* and *The Song of the Lark*.

In any event, two other admired features of the Harling home may be mentioned. First of all, although it is located in town technically, it is described as "like a little farm." It has a garden, a barn, a windmill, an orchard, and grazing land. Hence, if it is evident that if the other two idealized households are those of people close to the land, this is not far removed. Significantly enough, when Jim tries to define the "basic harmony" between Antonia and Mrs. Harling, he notes that both enjoy "digging in the earth." Secondly, the Harlings have some appreciation of the arts. Almost all play the piano, and Mrs. Harling tells them the stories of the operas from which she plays arias. They also have dancing and story-telling. Likewise in the Burden home, Grandfather read from the Bible, and Jim read for his grandmother a chapter from *The Prince of the House of David*, as well as works such as *Robinson Crusoe*, by himself. On Saturday nights, Otto would sing cowboy songs or tell tales of adventure. Finally, when years later Jim visits Antonia's house, two of her children will offer musical selections. To sum up, the good household as represented three times in *My Antonia* is one that is well stocked with provisions and efficiently run by a strong, competent, motherly woman who has kept close to nature by farming or gardening and who fosters some interest in cultural pursuits.

As for the hired girls, with whom this section is concerned, the move to town is at first glance a matter of joyous liberation. Lena, who in torn and ragged dress used to herd her father's cattle, now has nice clothes and a room of her own with a carpet. Antonia, too, who was hired out by Ambrosch to work as a field hand, is now learning to sew, to dance, and to speak English well. Up at the hotel Tiny Soderball is being given little gifts of perfume, handkerchiefs, and gloves by the kindly, generous salesmen, and is sharing these small luxuries with her friends. These immigrant girls are decent, hard-working young women, and it seems only fair that they should enjoy the very real advantages offered them by the town. Yet given Miss Cather's concept of the good life close to the soil, there is the possibility that the town may also offer certain dangers. Mrs. Harling fears lest Lena "go gadding about to dances" when she should be working and is not sure that the hotel "is a good place for a girl." Actually, as it turns out, neither of these girls will go beyond material success to become an ideal wife and mother like Mrs. Harling herself. Instead, like the hired men and Jim, they will end up individuals without strong human ties. Antonia, however, encounters the temptations of the town, at least for a time, under the sponsorship of the wise, capable, and sympathetic mistress of a happy, well-run household. This interlude will later be seen to have proved a fortunate transition.

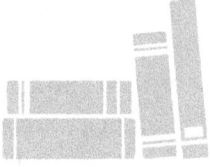

MY ANTONIA

TEXTUAL ANALYSIS

BOOK II: THE HIRED GIRLS - CHAPTERS 8-15

In late spring, the Vannis, an exotic-looking Italian trio, arrive in town and set up a dancing pavilion. From then on through the summer Black Hawk evenings are more exciting. Some nights the dance floor is reserved by the exclusive Progressive Euchre Club. Jim, however, prefers the Saturday night gatherings, when he can enjoy a whirl with Antonia, Lena, Tiny, and their friends. Indeed, even the boys from the Progressive Euchre Club sometimes slip in late and risk social criticism for a waltz with the country girls.

Black Hawk has an odd social system. The townsfolk look down snobbishly upon the hired girls who have taken jobs to help their families. Yet in contrast to these strong, glowing young immigrants, with their free, assured strides, the town girls are pale and listless. Never taking any exercise, they seem to move no muscles even when dancing and grow up round-shouldered and flat-chested. Even their economic advantage is not permanent. The country girls send wages home, pay off family mortgages, and eventually marry prosperous farmers. The proud American-born maidens sit home and contribute nothing. Some town boys find the vital hired girls attractive but lack the independence to marry them. Sylvester Lovett, for instance, the banker's son, is most attentive to Lena, but terrified of possible entanglements, he runs off with a rich widow. Jim regards such youths with scorn.

Less shy than before, Antonia loves to dance and cannot wait to get to the pavilion. One night Harry Paine, a town boy soon to be married, sees her home and boldly tries to kiss her. When she furiously objects, the lordly Mr. Harling comes down and tells her to give up the dances or leave his house. Antonia defends her behavior and declares that she has a right to some fun. Despite Mrs. Harling's angry objections, she goes to work for the notorious Wick Cutter.

Wick Cutter, libertine and swindler, hypocritically quotes moral maxims and is proud of his fussy, over-decorated house. He fights continually with his wife, a wild-eyed, red-faced woman with a passion for painting flowers on china. His one fear is that she will outlive him and inherit his property.

With Lena's help, Antonia dresses better, and wears plumed hats and high heeled shoes. After the Vannis leave, Jim refuses to join the upperclass Owl Club and is bored and discontented. Discouraged by Grandfather from visiting Jelinek's saloon, he slips out to the Firemen's Hall to meet his country friends. Lena makes every dance a dreamy waltz, but a whirl with Antonia is more exciting. Sometimes she is escorted by a glib train conductor, Larry Donovan. Another time Jim tries to kiss her, but she insists that he stay away from her and Lena and go on to college.

Jim graduates, a rather lonely valedictorian, and is warmly congratulated by Antonia. That summer he studies hard alone, but on a July Sunday he goes on a picnic with the country girls. They talk of their families and of their own plans. Antonia tells him that her father had not been forced to marry her peasant mother but had done so from a high sense of honor. Jim talks of a theory that Coronado explored as far north as Nebraska. At dusk the young people are startled at the effect of a huge plow silhouetted against the sun.

In August, the Cutters go out of town, but Antonia suspects a plot. Jim reluctantly stays the night at the house, and has a bloody battle with Wick in the dark. He is angry with Antonia for having involved him in the business. Jim wants no hero's bruises.

CHARACTER ANALYSIS: BOOK II, CHAPTERS 8-15

Jim Burden

In this section Jim is seen as the lonely outsider generally at odds with the town. When he rejects the Progressive Euchre Club and its successor, the Owls, and deliberately courts criticism by associating with the country girls, he is taking a strong stand against certain Black Hawk values.

Jim, it must be remembered, was not born in Black Hawk, or even in Nebraska. He arrived as a boy of ten from a distant and very different part of the United States. So from the first, he had seen more than a single way of living, unlike those who had grown up knowing only one small area, one small group, and one narrow set of conventions. In addition, having lived on the farm and known country people, he has a high regard for healthy outdoor activities and finds stifling the closed-in town houses with their shuttered parlors. It also seems to him that the town's disdain for open air and physical fitness is but one more manifestation of its mean, small-minded, negative thinking.

If Jim has known an older Virginia culture and also the freer life of the open prairie, he has also been more closely acquainted with immigrant groups than have been many of the townsfolk. Having witnessed the early struggles of the Shimerdas, he realizes how brave and patient these people have had to be. Having liked Antonia's gentle father and been deeply affected by his tragic death, he can never again look scornfully upon all foreigners as stupid and ignorant. Moreover, having long been friendly with Antonia herself, he is well aware of her lively intelligence, her willingness to work hard, and her warm-hearted generosity, as well as her glowing beauty and her keen enjoyment of life. He therefore cannot possibly accept without question the town's apparent assumption that native-born Americans are superior in every way to immigrants and should therefore not regard them as social equals.

Jim not only holds views at variance with those of most people of Black Hawk, he, in effect, openly avows them. He coolly turns down usually coveted invitations to join clubs run by the town's social set. As a high school senior, he coaxes Antonia, Lena, and the rest into the ice cream parlor. Even they know what this implies. Norwegian Anna, one of the more dignified girls in the group, makes them all be quiet when the principal drops in to buy bread. She knows that the whisper is going through town that Jim is sly or odd, ignoring the girls of his own set in favor of the vivacious immigrants. His determined stand has its consequences. He is often lonely and becomes bored and restless. At graduation, he is class valedictorian, but only his country friends and the Harlings gather around him to offer congratulations.

Jim thus is an independent youth, with the courage necessary to withstand popular disapproval. He is good in physical combat, too. When, at his grandmother's urging, he takes over guard duty at the Cutter house because Antonia suspects a ruse, he gives a good account of himself in the battle with the midnight intruder. Yet as he rushes home battered, bruised, and partially clad, he is petrified lest someone see him, spread the story and subject him to ridicule. The next morning, feeling weary and hurt, he is in no mood for Antonia's tearful gratitude. He is merely angry that she got him into this predicament. Jim may have his heroic side, but he is not one to glory in the role of knight errant.

Antonia Shimerda

Four aspects of Antonia's character are developed in this section. First of all, there is her exuberant delight in dancing. Her zest and sparkle make her a wonderful partner, and she is immediately popular. Dancing with her, says Jim, is an adventure. She does the schottische with sprightly grace and is always inventing new steps. Her eagerness to have fun at the pavilion while she can will cost her good position at the Harling's but it is one more proof that this girl loves life and will pursue its rewarding pleasures with unfeigned enthusiasm.

Secondly, she, too, like Jim, is an independent spirit. She likes the Harlings and is not by nature inclined to be bold or impertinent. Yet when the imperious Mr. Harling sets up what she considers unfair alternatives, she promptly gives her notice. Her going to work for Wick Cutter, a notorious seducer of young servants, is hardly a prudent move. But her assured announcement that she can take care of herself is further evidence of her habit of thinking and acting on her own initiative.

On the other hand, she is not lacking altogether in common sense as regards her amorous employer. When he makes some odd provisos about her remaining in the house alone while he and his wife are away, she shrewdly suspects that he may intend to return secretly and make unwelcome advances. Hitherto she has apparently justified her rash announcement that she could handle the situation. Now, however, she recognizes the more serious danger and does not let pride prevent her from seeking aid. Sensibly, she comes to Grandmother Burden, and with Jim's help she is saved from the fate that befell several of her predecessors in the Cutter household.

Finally, there is her loyalty and devotion to Jim. She wants him to have his chance to get further education and to have a great career in the world. She therefore encourages him constantly to go on with his studies. Although she enjoys dancing with him, she will not let him get himself romantically involved with her or with any of her friends. She is particularly concerned about the lovely, yielding Lena, whom she knows Jim finds attractive. Sternly she warns him to behave himself. Otherwise she will go to Mrs. Burden. For the most part, however, she praises warmly his accomplishments, such as his graduation speech, shares with him her precious memories of her father, and keeps assuring him that he is destined for success.

Mrs. Harling

The quick temper of Mrs. Harling flares up in this section. Having accepted her husband's ultimatum that Antonia must give up the dances or leave their employ, Mrs. Harling is hurt and angry when the girl decides to leave. Ironically enough she had become fond of Antonia because they were somewhat similar personalities. Both, for instance, were independent.

Now when the younger woman's strong will clashes with her own, she is, humanly enough, furious. Subsequently, when Jim tries to defend Antonia, Mrs. Harling becomes annoyed with him too. Yet she is not one to hold grudges indefinitely. She comes to Jim's graduation and brings him a silk umbrella. Eventually, too, she becomes reconciled with Antonia.

Grandfather Burden

Here Grandfather shows his conservatism as a Baptist deacon by letting Jelinek know that he does not want Jim seen around the Bohemian's saloon. When Jim delivers his Commencement oration, he is proud of the boy, according to Antonia, but does not tell him so. Although he has some misgivings, he does listen to Mrs. Harling's plea that young Jim be permitted to go away alone to college.

Grandmother Burden

Worried lest Jim acquire a poor reputation and grieved that he is sneaking out to the Firemen's Hall dances, Grandmother sheds tears. Unwilling to cause her further distress, Jim gives up the dances. When Antonia comes to her with her fears about Cutter's designs, she is sympathetic and helpful. First she suggests that Jim help keep watch. Later, after the battle, she goes with Antonia to help her pack. At that time she also soothes the irate Mrs. Cutter, who has learned of the trick attempted by her wily husband.

Wick Cutter

First encountered when he took over all the possessions of Russian Peter, Wick here turns up as the would-be seducer of

Antonia. Both actions suggest a vicious individual, but just as *My Antonia* plays down conventional heroics, so it subtly avoids the usual representation of villainy. Because of his long-term war with his wife, complete with cruel but outlandish practical jokes, Cutter is essentially a comic character. Miss Cather furnishes details that make him appear ridiculous. For example, he talks so much about his neat lawn that mischievous lads enjoy throwing dead cats over his fence. Again, he is afraid that his wife will outlive him and thus get his property for her relatives. Gleefully she insists that this is probable thanks to his dissolute habits. This alarms him, and he starts working out feverishly with dumbbells. Finally, his scheme to ruin Antonia fails, and he must sneak for a time out of town with his face striped with court-plaster, his arm in a sling.

Mrs. Cutter

A big, wild-looking woman, with long curved teeth, Mrs. Cutter is almost as bizarre a character as her husband. Nodding ceaselessly, she sometimes appears almost mad. Yet she affects a reserved manner when she pays calls in her gray brocade and plumed bonnet. Like Wick, she too has a strange sense of humor. She seems to take a peculiar pleasure out of sending him anonymous clippings about erring husbands, but she leaves the newspapers from which she cut them in plain sight for him to find. To shame Wick into giving her more money she once threatens to go around town soliciting orders for painted china, but gives this up in chagrin when he acts merely pleased. When Antonia makes herself dress like those of town social leaders, Mrs. Cutter is secretly delighted. Later outraged when Wick puts her on the wrong train so that he can return to surprise Antonia, she returns home half-hysterical, but vows to make him pay for having so wronged her. Actually, both Cutters seem almost to relish their weird hostilities.

BRIGHT NOTES STUDY GUIDE

Comment: Book II, Chapters 8-15

Again in this section material can be traced to the youthful experiences of the author. For one thing, Willa Cather, like Jim, delivered a commencement address, and she, too, seems to have been an independent young person unwilling to follow blindly any narrowly conventional course. In describing the social attitudes of Black Hawk, she also undoubtedly was drawing upon her memories of life in Red Cloud.

Although her portraits of the odd, squabbling Cutters are developed with considerable artistry, she based them upon actual individuals, E. C. Bentley and his wife. Bentley was Red Cloud's first money-lender and charged fantastic rates of interest. He spent a great deal on himself, but was miserly toward his wife (Bennett, 82-3).

Also based upon fact is the incident in which Antonia is peremptorily ordered by Mr. Harling to remain away from future dances. Mr. Miner found the son of a woman he disliked paying court to one of his hired girls. He forbade her to see the boy again, and the maid quit in anger (Bennett, 69). Here it is interesting to observe how Miss Cather altered the whole **episode** to bring out certain ideas.

First of all, the original young man proved not at all objectionable to the girl he was seeing home. In the novel, however, the youth tries to force his attentions upon Antonia. This points up the double standards of town boys, because this same Harry Paine is slated to marry quite profitably one of his own set two days later. Of course, it also indicates Antonia's sense of propriety, her independent spirit, and her feeling that she is entitled to at least some fun out of life.

These chapters in general take a long critical look at the American small town as Willa Cather knew it before the century's turn. With its shaded sidewalks and fenced-in lawns, Black Hawk (or Red Cloud) presents a neat, pleasant appearance. Yet Jim, and probably the novelist, found life there rather dull and dreary. His one haven was the Harling home, which, we recall, was like a "little farm," run by those who had been "farming people." Otherwise, whatever is interesting or entertaining seems to come from outside, from the traveling men, from Blind d'Arnault, from the Vannis. Much is made of how uneventful summer nights were in town before the pavilion was opened.

The town, however, is not only unexciting. It is narrow-minded and snobbish. Before the Vannis came, the young people could not even laugh aloud without criticism, and the lads from the Progressive Euchre Club will be censured by their set if seen dancing with the hired girls on Saturday night.

The novelist's feelings about such a rigid caste system seem to be quite vehement. At times, in fact, there is more argument than narrative in this section. Walking along the quiet streets at night, Jim thinks of all the envy and sadness in the small flimsy houses. He sees the fearful inhabitants as forever dodging, denying, and cutting corners on work merely to have more time for gossip. To him they are like frightened mice scurrying through the dark.

By contrast, the country girls are seen to typify all that is lacking in the supercilious town. They are strong and healthy, whereas the town girls are stoop-shouldered and listless. They are working hard and using their earnings constructively to help their families pay off farms. Meanwhile their town counterparts sit around gossiping meanly in stuffy parlors.

These independent young women have every quality to attract young men, but the town boys are too spineless to meet the challenge. They are short-sighted, too, for the country girls will later make good homemakers and prove to be excellent wives and mothers. At one point Frances Harling accuses Jim of being a romantic and glamorizing the country girls. Frances, of course, is based upon Willa Cather's close friend, Carrie Miner. Was this, by any chance, a point on which they actually differed? Certainly, Miss Cather has sometimes been criticized for idealizing her immigrant heroines and making them seem nobler than the originals probably were. It would appear that the author was well aware of the charge. Yet she still seems to agree with Jim that the Antonias, with their natural kindliness and true hearts, were far more "real women" than the pale town girls who dreamed of "brand new little houses with best chairs that must not be sat upon."

Throughout the work, in fact, as we have seen, Willa Cather is contrasting ways of life. This is probably the reason why she goes to such lengths to prevent our being overly impressed with the wickedness of Wick Cutter, although he is undoubtedly villainous. In the usual romances of the period when *My Antonia* first appeared, much more would have been made of the rather brutal fight between Jim and Wick, especially since it was a matter of saving the heroine from an unpleasant fate. Yet, as she did in the **episode** of the snake fight, the novelist refuses to maintain the lofty heroic tone. Jim fleeing across town in his night clothing, fearful of being seen, is hardly the champion accepting acclaim with dignity. Cutter, too, appears almost pathetic scurrying to the depot with his face all bandaged. In *My Antonia*, there is a very real, very serious conflict between good and evil, and there is genuine heroism held up to admiration. When Jim battles town prejudice and refuses to treat his country friends as social inferiors, he subjects himself to general disapproval and must endure months of loneliness. When Antonia speaks up for what she regards as her rights, she loses her job. This type of moral victory is much more significant in the Cather works than that of striking down a snake or beating up a fatuous libertine.

Yet despite its emphasis here on social criticism, this section does introduce two new dramatic elements. The more frequent references to Lena's soft, clinging manner and willing kisses suggest a possible future relationship between her and Jim. To some extent, of course, Antonia and Lena seem to represent opposing forces as regards the boy's future. Ironically enough Jim angrily denounces town boys who lack the discrimination or the courage to choose country girls as wives. Yet Antonia insists that he go away and leave them all in order to make something of his life. The second item worth noting is a brief and casual mention of the fact that Antonia sometimes goes to dances with a smooth-talking train conductor, Larry Donovan. He will later play a crucial part in her story.

In earlier sections certain scenes were noted, such as the Old Hata and Christmas Day incidents, that exemplify Willa Cather's skilled interweaving of joy and sorrow to produce rich emotional effects. Here there is the same artistry as the country girls meet to congratulate Jim after his graduation. Having just delivered an oration that he with all due modesty considers "very good," Jim doubtless feels a certain elation. Moreover, Mrs. Harling, who has been irked with him because of his defense of Antonia, has come to the exercises, followed his speech closely, and praised him heartily. She has also given him a silk umbrella, with his name on the handle.

Afterwards he walks home alone, but in the moonlight waiting for him are Antonia, Lena, and Norwegian Anna.

Antonia is most enthusiastic, and the others are friendly. Yet there is a note of sadness, too. Jim's eloquent talk reminds Antonia of her beloved father, and the boy admits that he too thought of Mr. Shimerda and dedicated his oration to him. There is also Anna's rather wistful remark that she "always wanted to go to school." These three likeable girls in their white dresses will never have the chance to go through high school, much less go on to college as Jim will presently. Yet they generously rejoice in his triumph and loyally wish him well. Recalling the event later Jim states that no later success ever pulled so at his heartstrings. As in the Old Hata scene nothing much actually happens here on the surface. Three girls stop to pay respects to an old friend who has just graduated. Yet with its setting of moonlight on maple trees, its whiteclad trio, and its brief but revealing bits of dialogue, this becomes a curiously moving encounter.

Even more memorable, however, is the chapter on the picnic, for it seems to sum up and integrate several **themes** developed in the story up to this point. Jim's delight in his early morning swim recalls his first joyful discovery of the Nebraska countryside. Later Antonia talks of her father's happier life of companionship and good talk in Bohemia, and her words bring back to mind the whole tragedy of the gentle Mr. Shimerda. As the day goes on, the plaintive remarks of the girls again point up the disadvantage of their limited schooling, the hard struggles of their immigrant mothers, and the problem of providing for big families. And Jim's provocative theory about the Coronado expedition that may have reached Nebraska casts a romantic aura over the outing.

Finally, there is the startling effect of the plow in the distance looming up black and huge in the sunset. It seems to be a symbol of all those solid farm families, whose daughters are Jim's friends. This magnificent descriptive passage is often cited as illustrating Miss Cather's style at its best. The scene also marks the end of Jim's Nebraska boyhood. As the sun goes down, the mood is one of exaltation.

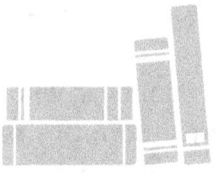

MY ANTONIA

TEXTUAL ANALYSIS

BOOK III: LENA LINGARD

At the university in Lincoln, Jim is privileged to have as Latin teacher and personal friend Gaston Cleric, a brilliant young New England scholar and poet sent West for his health. Cleric opens new realms of ideas, but Jim still finds himself vividly recalling the country people he used to know.

Only recently established, the college itself has a young optimistic spirit. Many of the students are poor farm boys, and the faculty includes ministers in hard straits and eager youths from graduate schools. Since there are no dormitories, Jim rents rooms from an elderly pioneer couple. He enjoys setting up his study and having Cleric drop in for visits. He later recalls especially the instructor's wonderful recital from memory of long passages from Dante's *Divine Comedy*.

One March evening Jim reads in Virgil's *Georgics* the sad observation that "the best days are the first to flee." He is also impressed with Virgil's idea of being the first to bring the Muse into his own "patria" or region. Then, answering a knock, he is startled to see Lena Lingard, poised and lovely in a conservative outfit of dark blue. She now has her own dress business in Lincoln. (Mrs. Burden knew this fact but did not write of it to Jim.) Lena tells him that Antonia is practically engaged to Larry Donovan, whom the Harlings and others mistrust. Lena reminds Jim that once Antonia likes someone, she tends to be fiercely loyal.

When Lena leaves, Jim decides that it is girls like her who make all poetry possible. After her call, they go often together to one-night performances of touring shows. They see *Rip Van Winkle, Shenandoah, Robin Hood,* and eventually a lavishly staged production of *Camille*, with an aging star who moves both to tears. Recalling his ecstatic walk home along lilac-scented paths, Jim the man decides that whenever Camille is produced, the month is always April.

Jim often meets Lena downtown, but she insists that he keep her out of sweet shops. She speaks English well, having even mastered the stilted phrases of her trade that please small-town ladies. At her lodgings Jim meets her devoted landlord, old Colonel Raleigh, and another admirer, Ordinsky, a violin teacher who worries lest Jim's intentions not be honorable. Jim reassures him, and they become friends.

Compared with Lena, Jim's studies begin to seem uninteresting. Cleric thereupon urges Jim to go on to Harvard, where the instructor will be teaching next. Trying vainly to convince himself that the move is best for everyone, Jim bids farewell to Lena. She is saddened but is at least grateful to have been his first sweetheart. At this time she also tells him that she will never marry. She has seen too much of the hardships of family life as a young girl, and wants to retain the freedom she has worked so hard to attain. Shortly thereafter Jim leaves to join Cleric in Boston.

CHARACTER ANALYSIS: BOOK III

Jim Burden

The implication has been evident in the book up to this point that Jim is a good student. Several times he is mentioned as reading various books as a small boy, and he was able to give English lessons to the Shimerda girls when he was ten or eleven. He was valedictorian of his class and apparently delivered an original oration that much impressed those who heard it. It is therefore not surprising that he would attract the attention of the inspiring young teacher from the East. The same enthusiasm that characterized his response to the beauty of the prairie and the goodness and charm of the immigrant girls shows itself here in his initial delight in the new areas of learning to which Cleric introduces him.

Yet Jim also makes at this time some interesting and important discoveries about himself. For one thing he is astonished at the deep impression which his early experiences with Antonia, Russian Peter, and the two hired men have made upon him. This discovery startles him, for he has been stimulated by Cleric's passion for learning. He thus expects his own small past to lose significance as he comes up against the far more momentous happenings described in the classics. Actually, however, the more he reaches out for the wonders of antiquity, attempting apparently to be totally absorbed in them as he once was in the boundless plains of waving red grass, the more he is again vividly conscious of the extent to which he has been affected by his boyhood adventures.

He, therefore, half-reluctantly concedes that he will never make a scholar. Scholarship, he feels, demands that an individual be able to lose himself among things that are essentially impersonal. Jim, for his part, will be thoroughly satisfied only when he concerns himself with what he knows directly. Curiously enough, Antonia, who speculates several times about Jim's future throughout the early part of the book, never sees him as a teacher. She sees him as a doctor or a lawyer, who will someday be as rich as Mr. Harling. It may also be recalled that in the Introduction the narrator mentions that Jim has succeeded as counsel for the railroad because he loves "with a personal passion" the country through which the trains pass.

It is therefore possible that he is more affected by Cleric himself with his bursts of poetic imaginative talk than by the knowledge that Cleric imparts. Certainly, when Lena reenters his life, he loses interest in his books. Why linger over poetry when the very inspiration for poetry is so close at hand?

Is Jim in love with Lena? Speaking of Colonel Raleigh, Ordinsky, and himself, he says that all three are in love with her. Certainly he likes her. He enjoys going to the theatre with her. He likes to share Sunday breakfasts with her, play with her dog Prince, and talk over old times and mutual friends. With her around he finds it hard to concentrate on more prosaic matters, and herself she states that she is his "first sweetheart." Yet he cannot have been passionately involved to any great extent. Unlike the romantic Armand in Camille, he seems to suffer no heartbreak at the thought of deserting Lena for Harvard. He finds it hard to break the news to her, because he senses rightly that she will be sad. Yet he did not rush to her defense when Cleric called her "perfectly irresponsible."

Jim is called a romantic by both the narrator and the astute Frances Harling. This description does not necessarily mean, however, that he is going to be an ardent lover in the usual sense. When he is in Lincoln, he likes Cleric and Lena; but whenever he is excited intellectually, he reverts to Jake, Otto, and Russian Peter, who now stand out "strengthened and simplified" in his mind. In later life he will remain away from Antonia for some twenty years lest finding her worn and beaten might destroy some few last illusions. Some memories, he claims, are realities, and as such are superior to anything that one may ever again experience. It would thus seem that Jim derives more from his ideas of people than from the people themselves. Hence he can probably walk away from the lovely Lena with only limited regret, yet cherish for years the precious memory of her slow, "renunciatory" good-bye kiss.

Lena Lingard

This charming young career woman is pictured, generally, as a real credit to her immigrant people. She is, first of all, extremely capable. Brought up in poverty with little or no formal education, she has become a successful dressmaker. She speaks English well and is adept at using all the standard polite phrases that induce wealthy women to become her clients. She has a genuine flair for design and now runs her own shop and hires young girls to help with the sewing. She is also extremely independent; and independence, as we have seen, is a much admired trait in this novel. She has gone off by herself and set up her shop in a town where she must make new business contacts and new friends. She refuses to let Jim pay for her ticket when they go to the theatre. In addition, she makes it clear that although she has had proposals of marriage, she has no intention of ever accepting any. This would appear to characterize her as an individualistic young woman in any age. In 1918, when *My Antonia* first appeared, it would seem even more startling.

Lena is also kind and gracious, and numbers among her admirers many different types. The lonely old Southern colonel is pleased with her gentle manners and asks her more than once to be his wife. The rather violent musician, Ordinsky, praises her for that warmth of feeling that he finds seldom among the more phlegmatic Nebraskans. Jim, too, reacts favorably to her because of her sympathetic understanding, never more in evidence than when she gracefully accepts his decision to leave.

Like Jim, she is capable of enthusiasm. He finds it always a pleasure to go with her to the theatre, for to her everything onstage is both wonderful and true. When the heroine of Camille nobly agrees to give up her lover at his father's request, Lena sobs. And when the young French hero, not understanding the sacrifice, denounces Marguerite bitterly, Lena cringes and covers her face. She is thus quite different from the "unimpressionable" woman who Jim later marries.

Yet despite her thoughtfulness and her sympathetic nature, Lena is only generous up to a point. She will pay her own way at the theatre and tactfully spare Jim embarrassment. She will gladly sew the torn coat of poor Ordinsky and listen patiently to the old stories of the Colonel. She will send later a substantial wedding present to Antonia and she will gladly use some of her money to build a new house for her mother and even furnish it. She will not, however, sacrifice herself for others in the way a Mrs. Harling or an Antonia will. She likes good times and enjoys a casual romantic fling. She does not want a husband who might be ill-tempered or children who would need constant care. Gaston Cleric describes her as pretty but "irresponsible." This charge is not entirely fair, in view of her concern for her mother. Yet it is true that she firmly refuses to accept the responsibilities of a home and children.

Gaston Cleric

This brilliant but sickly Latin professor from New England is an intense, dominating personality. A man of moods, he is sometimes silent and withdrawn, sometimes brusquely sarcastic. When lecturing at his best, however, he is wonderfully imaginative. He is passionately interested in his subject and conveys the excitement of reliving ancient times to his students. Visiting the antique temples at Paestum in Italy, he is so enraptured that he remains there all night and ruins his health. He is not, however, unaware of events in Lincoln. He takes into account Jim's inability to study, with Lena present to distract him, and takes the trouble to write to the young man's grandfather to ask that he be permitted to transfer to Harvard. Jim is surprised that his grandfather agrees so readily. The question is: does the astute teacher, much concerned about the future of his promising student, tell Mr. Burden enough about the lad's friendship with Lena to insure an affirmative reply? The novel does not settle this point, but the possibility is intriguing.

Antonia Shimerda

In this section Antonia plays no direct part, but she is more than once mentioned by Lena and Jim. On her first visit, Lena says that Antonia continues her enthusiastic expectations regarding Jim's future. She is telling everyone that he will be richer than

Mr. Harling. Mrs. Harling has forgiven her because little Nina is so fond of her. Yet in view of Antonia's former difficulties with her autocratic employer, is there more than mere loyalty in her hope that her champion will one day outshine in wealth that imposing gentleman? Antonia can be stubborn.

This refusal to yield to others on what seems a matter of fairness is also evident in her idolizing of Larry Donovan. Mrs. Harling and her other friends make every attempt to warn her that he is unreliable. She believes in him, however, and will listen to nothing that might discredit him.

Mrs. Harling

Despite her grievance against Antonia, Mrs. Harling magnanimously renews the friendship. She also tries to help the girl by warning her about the worthless train conductor. Incidentally, the same shrewdness that enabled her to take the measure of the blustering Ambrosch is evident in her reactions to Donovan.

Comment: Book III

Willa Cather graduated from Red Cloud High School in 1890 and went on to the University of Nebraska, founded in 1869. Her description of Jim's life there draws heavily on her own experiences. The study that the young man fixes up for himself, for instance, recalls her own accommodations as a student; and the whole picture of the fledgling university is that of her Alma Mater as she remembered it. The original for Gaston Cleric seems mainly to have been Herbert Bates, a New England teacher and poet who gave her great encouragement there. Yet the portrait may well combine traits of several stimulating professors who helped her launch her career.

Having both Jim and Lena enjoy the theatre gives Miss Cather a chance to work in more about one of her major interests. While at the University in Lincoln, she earned money by writing drama criticism for the local paper. She saw every play that came to town and was known for her severe comments (Bennett, 184).

In the chapter wherein Jim alludes to plays he has enjoyed, she lists a number of notable productions that came to Nebraska for one-night stands during her student days. Jim mentions, for instance, *Rip Van Winkle*. Starring Joseph Jefferson, a member of an old theatrical family, this was a very famous play of the era. Also noted is *The Count of Monte Cristo*. This romantic play about an escaped French prisoner who poses as a nobleman provided the greatest starring role for James O'Neill, the father of Eugene O'Neill, the well-known playwright.

Jim describes in considerable detail, however, one play in particular, Camille, indicating that at the time the leading actress was well past her prime. When Miss Cather attended the performance in question, she actually saw Clara Morris, an actress much acclaimed for this part, who was originally discovered by Augustin Daly, one of the most influential of American theatre managers. In her original account of the show, written during college days, Miss Cather praised the star's "terrible and relentless" realism but found the play itself "awful" (Bennett, 185). The long account in *My Antonia* certainly suggests that the acting was forceful, but Jim and Lena are far less critical of the play itself than was the young Miss Cather. Her report of their enthusiastic response is done with gentle, tolerant humor and with a perspective gained over the years. Compare the handling of this incident with Jim's story of the snake in Book I. In each we are constantly given both the boy's reaction at the time and the man's comments on the incident. Is this an effective way of handling such material? Frank O'Connor, the famed present-day Irish writer, makes good use of it also in his short stories.

Incidentally, we often find in the works of Willa Cather hints or suggestions that are most interesting yet are never fully worked out. As a novelist, Miss Cather never felt obliged to tell her readers everything she knew about her characters. She seems to have expected them to use a little imagination.

Two examples of this have already been indicated in the previous character analysis pages. Why does Antonia pointedly compare Jim with Mr. Harling? And what does Gaston Cleric include in his letter to Grandfather? Two further questions of this type, however, may be raised. For one thing, there is the matter of the romance between Jim and Lena. Certain passages suggest that it was more than merely an innocent flirtation, but the reader is left free to draw his own conclusions.

It is also worth speculating as to why, among all the plays she witnessed, Miss Cather chose to include so complete an account of Camille. Why not, for instance, *Rip Van Winkle* or *The Count of Monte Cristo*? Camille is, of course, a famous work, which would be familiar to readers. Those who had not seen the play might well have had some acquaintance with the opera La Traviata, which tells the same story. This would be helpful since the chapter is intended to point up the enthusiastic response of two impressionable, rather unsophisticated young people, and readers would probably know enough about the scenes in question to understand why Lena might weep uncontrollably or cower as if struck. In the Introduction the narrator suggested a vital distinction between romantic people who are capable of enthusiasm and those who are coldly insensitive. A scene like this once more places Jim and Lena squarely in the first, much favored group.

Yet it is tempting to explore a little further the idea that there may have been additional reasons for giving so much attention to Camille. Interestingly enough, although often Jim seems to serve as spokesman for the novelist, she has given him reactions to the play that were not quite those she expressed as a young drama critic. He is naively charmed by it all; she called it an "awful" show. We have seen that she elsewhere alters remembered material for a specific literary purpose. For instance, she adapted the incident of Mr. Miner and the maid in such a way as to bring out Antonia's independent spirit and the town boy's dubious standards. So it would seem reasonable to assume that Miss Cather may have had something more in mind when she handled the Camille **episode** in a special way.

Camille, a highly emotional drama, has a very young man of fairly high birth, Armand, fall passionately in love with Marguerite, a charming, worldly woman, notorious for illicit affairs. She is known as Camille, or the Lady of the Camellias, because she favors that flower. Because she is ill with tuberculosis, Armand persuades Marguerite to go away with him to the country, where she may recover her health. They are happy there together, until the boy's father, tearful lest his son's future be wrecked by such an association, secretly talks the good-hearted Camille into giving him up. Unaware of her noble sacrifice, Armand berates her bitterly, causing her intense suffering. After this she becomes increasingly weaker from consumption. As she lies dying, the penitent Armand, told all by his father, comes to see her. After a tearful reunion, she dies content.

Note here the curious parallels, and the equally significant variations. Jim, like Armand, is a rather unsophisticated young man of quite an upper-class family by Nebraska standards. He was, after all, invited to join the exclusive clubs in Black Hawk. Lena is somewhat older than he and already much more experienced in affairs of the heart. While Miss Cather always handles the matter reticently, there is every indication that Lena has rather flexible moral standards. Seeing her more often, Jim becomes very fond of the girl. He can, in fact, think of nothing else. Since he is an orphan, no father can intervene; but Gaston Cleric, concerned about the youth's future, certainly takes steps to remove him from the distractions offered by the "irresponsible" Lena. Lena is saddened by the parting.

Here, however, the similarities end. Miss Cather may be sympathetic to "romantics" who respond with feeling to whatever wonders they experience, such as the autumn prairie, a pathetic suicide, a strange sunset image of a plow, or a moving drama. Yet she generally takes a stand against the sentimental **cliches** of earlier fiction. She is a twentieth-century American writer who has little patience with the melodramatic nonsense that dazzles the emotions while making no sense whatsoever as a valid representation of life.

Here, in effect, she gives us two versions of the Camille story, the sentimental and a more realistic modern treatment. The one on stage tears at the hearts of sensitive young spectators but bears little relation to their own subsequent behavior.

Jim may well be in love with the amiable Lena, but he is also ambitious enough to appreciate Cleric's argument. The teacher, for his part, does not set up some kind of absurd misunderstanding by going to Lena and insisting that she make a showy gesture certain to confuse and embitter her young admirer. Lena herself is made unhappy by Jim's decision - her good-bye kiss is a slow "renunciatory" one. Yet Miss Cather does not have her suffering from some conveniently fatal malady that will guarantee a deathbed scene eulogizing her as grievously wronged. Lena has had other loves and will presumably have more in the future. She will also go on doing quite well in the dressmaking business.

It must always be remembered that when it first appeared *My Antonia* was hardly the conventional novel. It lacked the standard love story and it had nothing resembling the usual plot formulas. Its whole line was to reject false, ostentatious heroics in favor of the more solid, long-term heroism of those who lived relatively quietly and endured hardships bravely, thus strengthening their own characters and contributing something to their country by running good farms or decent businesses and raising fine big families. Viewed in this light, the Camille incident seems most aptly chosen to contrast the old style of writing with the new.

Finally, the two quotations from Virgil given at the start of this section are unusually apt. The one about the best days which are quickly over recalls the elegiac, or sad, note struck in the Introduction, where Jim and the narrator look back on the "adventure" of their childhood. Willa Cather seems to have felt very strongly that youth was the most glorious period, the "best days" of a person's life. Then, if ever, one had the stimulating and rewarding experiences that would be remembered gratefully all the rest of his life. This idea clearly underlies *My Antonia*. Certainly Jim constantly suggests that nothing that happened to him as a man compared with his "best days" in Nebraska, and Miss Cather drew the material for most of her own successful books from her early life in and around Red Cloud.

The second quotation about being the first to bring the Muse, or the light of literature, to one's "patria" is also interesting. Willa Cather, although she lived elsewhere in later life, seems to have felt always that she belonged in a special way to the prairie country. This was her neighborhood, her "patria," and in her stories she gives literary status to the region and its people. She immortalizes Nebraska just as Virgil praised his native countryside, near Mincio, in the *Georgics*.

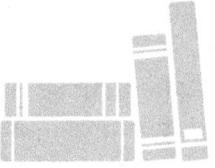

MY ANTONIA

TEXTUAL ANALYSIS

BOOK IV: THE PIONEER WOMAN'S STORY

....

Graduated from Harvard after two years, Jim comes home before starting law school. Frances Harling is now married, but his grandparents seem unchanged. People talk pityingly of Antonia. Having gone off to marry Donovan, she was deserted by him and now has an illegitimate child. Jim wonders why she could not have done so well as Tiny or Lena.

The town also sneers at Tiny, who went to Seattle to open a hotel for sailors. Looking back, the elder Jim admits that then no one could have predicted her later history of dangerous but profitable ventures.

After the gold strike in Alaska, she makes the difficult journey to Dawson City, opening there a restaurant and later another hotel. Having taken care of a fatally injured Swedish prospector, she falls heir to his claim. After ten hard years of mining and real estate deals, she returns rich to San Francisco. Meeting her in 1908, Jim finds her a slight, severe looking woman who cares only about money. Lena has joined her, still gossiped about but cautious enough. She sees to it that Tiny is always well dressed but sends her sizable bills. Tiny, who used to dance gaily, now limps, having lost three toes because of frostbite in Alaska. She is not very excited over her success. In fact, she no longer seems much interested in anything.

Back in town, Jim sees a large framed picture of Antonia's baby in the photographer's window. How like her not to be ashamed of the child. Jim still wonders angrily how she could have gone off with the lordly, self-pitying conductor. To find out more, he drives out to see the Widow Steavens, noting with pleasure how the open prairie he knew now boasts many prosperous farms.

The Widow Steavens relates how happy Antonia was before the ill-fated trip and how eagerly she sewed her trousseau. Even Ambrosch was moved to give her plated silver and three hundred dollars. Tricked and then abandoned, she returned home pregnant after a month. Never going into town, even to see a dentist, she herded Ambrosch's cattle until December and then, without help, bore her child. Ambrosch nastily suggested drowning it, thus evoking an angry warning from the Widow. Antonia, however, loved her baby just as much as if she had been married.

Jim meets Antonia in the fields. She is worn and thin but still vital. They talk of Mr. Shimerda and of Cleric's recent death. Jim is leaving for good, but to her he will seem near as does her father. She would never like living in a city. Jim says that he would like to have had her as sweetheart, wife, mother, or sister. As the moon rises, he holds her strong brown hands, thinking that hers is a genuine woman's face. Most are only shadows. Promising to return, he walks back alone, hearing from the past a laughing boy and girl.

CHARACTER ANALYSIS: BOOK IV

Jim Burden

In the previous section, Jim spoke of his discovery that as he read more of the classics the country people he had known as a boy stood out "strengthened and simplified" just as the plow had seemed to stand out against the sun. He then added that they were so alive in him that he seldom wondered whether they were alive elsewhere. In other words, Jim has such vivid memories of these friends of his youth that they go on being part of his life long after he has ceased to see them in the flesh. Among those he mentioned earlier were Jake, Otto, and Russian Peter. He hadn't seen or heard from any of them since he started to go to high school. Yet these old friends, or rather their images, accompany him in his new experiences and seem very much alive in him.

Jim throughout the work is a rather lonely individual, often the outsider. Hence these memory friends mean a great deal to him. In the Introduction, when the narrator first talks of Jim and Antonia, she says, "His mind was full of her that day." As a lad he walks the Black Hawk streets at night, solitary and aloof: as a man he travels on trains through the West, putting distance between himself and a loveless marriage. Thanks, however, to his romantic disposition, he can draw spiritual strength or renewal of hope by mentally rejoining once more the reliable, unchanging old acquaintances "strengthened and simplified" in his consciousness to represent solid, homely virtues.

Once we understand generally how Jim regards these remembered figures, we can better appreciate his reaction here to Antonia's misfortune. She has been good to him over the years and has praised him extravagantly to others. They have, in fact, been fairly close friends. Yet when he hears that she has been deserted and disgraced and is back on the farm drudging for Ambrosch, his feeling is not profound sympathy but bitter disappointment. He cannot forgive her for having exposed herself to the pity of others. He has his mental picture of her as the joyous girl who used to race through the countryside with him and as the real woman, with "warm, sweet face... kind arms, and...true heart." This is his Antonia, and he does not want his vision destroyed. If Antonia is in actuality going to be a foolish girl who throws her love away on a worthless braggart, thus courting public scorn, he wants only to shut her out of his mind.

He relents somewhat when he sees her baby's picture in the photographer's window. As a young lad in Black Hawk, Jim had little respect for the townspeople. He regarded them as narrow-minded snobs, too terrified of gossip ever to think for themselves. The picture, however, a crayon enlargement in an expensive gilt frame, means that Antonia is not keeping her child hidden away, but is showing pride in her offspring. This gesture of independence helps to reestablish Jim's favorable image of Antonia. He is still disgusted with her for her folly, but at least he will go to see her.

When he subsequently meets her after hearing the full story from the Widow Steavens, he quickly responds to her friendly interest and tells her all about himself. Then he assures her that when he was away he thought of her often. He would, in fact, have liked to have her as sweetheart, wife, mother, or sister, "anything that a woman can be to a man." He then makes two highly significant statements. "The idea of you is a part of my mind," he says, and adds, "You really are a part of me." Before he leaves, he holds her hands, thinking of the past, and scans her face, which he intends always to "carry with" him. Then he leaves, almost believing that he is accompanied by the young, laughing Jim and Antonia.

There is no indication that he asks about her baby or her family, the state of her health, or her plans for the future. If he leaves in an exalted frame of mind, it is because he once more has "his" Antonia, a vital person with warm, brown hands and a grave, strong expression, whose kindly concern about his friends, his way of living, and his hopes, is pleasantly reassuring. If Jim's peace of mind depends much upon happy memories, this meeting renews treasured recollections of a happy childhood and provides material for future reveries. Even at the time he looks closely at her face to fix it firmly in his consciousness.

What then are we to make of his ardent declaration that he wishes he could have had her as sweetheart, wife, mother, or sister? It probably should be taken largely as a sincere but rather vague outburst of sentiment. There is no evidence that he ever seriously tried to court her. For that matter, where he now in earnest, they are both still young and unmarried. But for all his genuinely democratic urges, she is an unschooled Bohemian immigrant farm woman with an out-of-wedlock child, and he is a Virginia-born university student. They move in different circles, and both tacitly recognize the fact. Moreover, if he cannot really decide whether even in theory he would have liked her as wife, mother, or sister, he has no definite relationship in mind. All in all, the idea of Antonia is what Jim needs and wants.

Antonia Shimerda

The account given Jim by the Widow Steavens reveals much about Antonia. As a young girl in love, preparing for her wedding, she was joy personified Gaily she would use the Widow's sewing machine, "pedaling the life out of it, all the while singing merry Bohemian songs. As always she worked very hard determined to run a good home for her future husband. She regarded herself as a country girl and disliked having to live in a city but she went off with happy tears when Donovan wrote her to come. Everything in this part of her story points up Antonia's high spirits, unlimited energy, and eagerness to do things well.

After her unfortunate experience, she is "crushed and quiet" but not one to weep self-pityingly and demand that others sympathize. Neither does she go around angrily denouncing her betrayer or even sink into lethargy or despair. Unwilling to subject herself to the town's patronizing airs, she stays at home even when plagued by ulcerated teeth. So it is clear that she is sensitive about her loss of reputation. Yet she bears herself with dignity, exercises good control over her feelings, and patiently endures her mother's muttering and Ambrosch's surliness, as well as her other afflictions. She is more than ever a strong character.

She is also strong physically. During the months of her pregnancy, when many women would limit activities, she goes on doing heavy farm work. Right up to the end, she herds cattle, even during a December snowfall. Then at night she goes in alone to her room and "without a groan" bears her child. When the Widow Steavens is summoned by the flustered Mrs. Shimerda, Antonia calmly directs her where to find the proper soap.

Strong morally and physically, Antonia seems somehow to draw her extraordinary vigor from the land. More than once in this section does she speak of how much being close to the soil means to her. She is troubled when she learns that she may have to live in Denver, afraid that she will not be able to manage so well without chickens or a cow.

Upon her return, the Widow notes that when watching her cattle Antonia likes to be alone and sun herself on the grassy banks. Uncertain as to how long she may live, she recalls her happier childhood and enjoys the autumn. When Jim makes his visit, she declares that she would always feel lonely and miserable in a city. She wants to live and die where she knows every stack and tree and "where all the ground is friendly."

Despite all that she has suffered, Antonia retains her warm, loving interest in others. She is glad to talk things over with the Widow and has no harsh words to say about the man who tricked and deserted her. She loves her baby dearly, and has its picture taken and beautifully framed. No child, says the Widow, ever received better care. Finally, when Jim arrives, she receives him graciously and insists upon hearing all about his friends, his way of living and his plans. At that time she also indicates her determination to see her little daughter gets a good start.

In general, Antonia seems to look ahead more than does Jim. When he was in high school, she was always speculating about his future and urging him to go away and achieve success. After he left, she went on telling people that one day he would be richer than Mr. Harling. After her sad experience, she thinks of happier days with Jim and her father, and she tells her friend later that she is grateful that they had each other when they were small. Yet she is most interested in his hopes and dreams. She also has one of her own. She wants to give her child a better chance than she had. The Widow calls Antonia a "natural-born mother." As such, she has reason to anticipate a busy, useful life in the years to come.

The Widow Steavens

Although mentioned as being present at the Shimerda funeral and later as renting the Burden farm, the Widow is much more fully delineated in this section. She is another of Miss Cather's sturdy, independent, kindly farm women. Jim describes her as brown as an Indian, tall and strong. Mrs. Harling called her a good talker with an excellent memory. And she does, in fact, tell Antonia's story in lively fashion with dialogue and revealing details.

First of all, she is a warmly sympathetic person. She rejoices in Antonia's marriage prospects, lets her run her sewing machine, and teaches her hemstitching and other skills. When Antonia returns, abandoned and shamed, the Widow, far from snubbing her, drives over promptly. As she listens to the girl's tale of woe, she is so "heart-broke" that she cries "like a young thing."

The Widow is also a woman of spirit. Hearing of Antonia's misfortune, she wonders tartly why such a "bad one" as Lena Lingard can walk proudly in her silks and satins. She does admit, however, that Lena is good to her mother. She also praises Ambrosch for acting like a man when he gives Antonia the silver and the three hundred dollars. Yet she warns him in no uncertain terms when he later says something about putting the infant in the rainbarrel. "I pride myself," she tells Jim, "I cowed him." The good Widow probably did, for the baby waxes strong and healthy, and Ambrosch is expected to pick up its framed picture at the photographer's!

Larry Donovan

The character of the train conductor who seduces Antonia is only lightly sketched. Except for Antonia, who is fairly reticent, all who mention him are hostile. Lena says that she and others could relate "things" about him and implies that the Harlings do not like him. Jim calls him a "professional ladies' man." Elsewhere, Jim speaks of him scornfully as a "train-crew aristocrat" who will not even condescend to open a window for a passenger. Cultivating an air of "official aloofness," he changes his uniform as soon as his run comes to an end. He never talks much to men but gravely confides in women how sadly his merits are unappreciated by the railroad, which has yet to make him a passenger agent. Antonia quietly adds the information that he is dishonest. Discharged for allowing passengers to ride at lower than authorized rates, he sent for Antonia without letting her know the facts. He was ill, and she took care of him. Then when her money had all been spent, he left without a word. She believes that he has gone down into Old Mexico where many conductors cheat the inhabitants and thus get rich. This is the man Antonia used to talk of proudly as if he were president of the whole railroad.

Tiny Soderball

Of the three hired girls, whose story is told at some length, Tiny is the most aggressive and most daring. Except for her disastrous romance with Larry, Antonia remains in and around Black Hawk. Lena moves only to Lincoln, until summoned by Tiny to the West Coast. Tiny, however, the hotel waitress who danced trippingly and yet could always keep customers in their place, goes far afield. Venturing first to Seattle, she goes on to the wilds of Alaska. She has some goodness of heart, since she took care of the dying Swedish prospector. Yet she is also a shrewd, hard-headed business woman, as is evident from her successful operations in real estate and mining. In devoting her life, however, to the accumulation of wealth, she seems to have missed out on many deeper satisfactions. Were it not for Lena, she would not even dress like a woman of means. When Jim sees her, she is pleased with her achievements, but not much excited about them or anything else.

Comment: Book IV

This section consists of two separate stories. The one tells of Tiny Soderball's rise from hired girl in a Black Hawk hotel to a wealthy resident of San Francisco. The other describes the lamentable failure to Antonia's marriage plans and Jim's last meeting with her before going on to law school and settling in New York. Hitherto we have noted repeatedly that this novel avoids the usual or conventional form. It may be worthwhile at the point to consider how the different sections are related and how taken together they form an integrated study of life.

Book I, "The Shimerdas," shows the ideal farm household as developed over a fairly long period by the well-established American settlers. By contrast it also describes the prodigious handicaps with which the European immigrants start to achieve this good life. So awesome are the obstacles that a fine, intelligent man is driven to suicide. Yet a young people like Antonia and Ambrosch go bravely to work, and gradually their lot improves.

Book II, "The Hired Girls," moves the action to Black Hawk. Having given up their farm, the Burdens no longer represent Nebraska settlers at their most productive. The Harlings alone manage to bring into the town the happy, wholesome atmosphere of the farm. The country girls come into Black Hawk to work, and it is soon seen that the social lines are sharply drawn. Jim, however, having known an admirable farm set-up and having followed with admiration the hard-won progress of the immigrant group, refuses to accept the town's narrow standards. In defiantly adopting a democratic attitude and treating the hired girls as his equals, he in effect wagers that these vital, bright-eyed young women are capable of accomplishing at least as much as, and probably more than, those native-born Americans who scorn them as stupid, ignorant foreigners.

The next two books, "Lena Lingard" and "The Pioneer Woman's Story," provide impressive support for his contention. Here the town's delusions of superiority are dealt with on its own terms. Inasmuch as no evidence is forthcoming that the smug citizenry of Black Hawk demonstrated unusual talent or capability, the inescapable conclusion is that their claims to belong to an upper class rest mainly on the fact that they are better off financially than the immigrants. They have fussier houses and more expensive clothes. Their men have made good livings in various lines of business, and they therefore enjoy a certain prestige. Coming from foreign families, Tiny and Lena start with nothing but their own intelligence, energy, and determination. Lena becomes a fashionable dressmaker who can attract as admirers American men of substance. Tiny, by her own efforts, accumulates a considerable fortune. If Black Hawk rates people on the basis of their material progress, Lena and Tiny score highly for the country girls.

How then does Antonia fit into the debate? In some ways she never even approaches the records set by her two friends. Even her English retains a slight accent. Moreover, although she does avoid the unwanted attentions of Cutter and the impudent town lad, she encounters nothing but misery when she accepts a marriage proposal from a native-born trainman. Even when regarding her with some pity, the town would seem to have some cause to dismiss this immigrant girl as naively imprudent. Yet the next and climactic book, Cusack's Boys, gives her the last word. Eventually, after long years of painful struggle, she will achieve the economic level required for some respect from the town. It will be mentioned in passing that the school has its picnic each year on her farm. Yet she will have done even more in the end than Lena or Tiny, or for that matter than the type of townsfolk that so wearied Jim. For she with her happy home and many children will have gone on to a fuller, richer life, with far deeper satisfactions. Succeeding the Burdens and the Harlings, she will add those special admirable traits that were part of her European heritage. All three hired girls thus refute the town's claim to automatic superiority in the three final sections of *My Antonia*. Lena and Tiny make impressive material gains. Antonia does well materially but also proves at length morally and spiritually greater than those who looked down upon her and friends.

A second question that arises in connection with the fourth section is that of Antonia's involvement with Donovan. Hitherto Antonia has been a fair judge of character. She was not fooled by Wick Cutter or Lena, and she was outraged when the engaged young man tried to kiss her. She also seems to have had fairly strict standards. She may have liked to dance, but she was never one for casual love affairs. The Widow Steavens makes a sharp distinction between the "good" Antonia and the "bad" Lena.

Actually, we are safe in assuming that if Willa Cather leaves so much about this affair unexplained, she probably does not want it overemphasized. Taken generally, it serves several purposes. First of all, it plays up the contaminating element of the town. Everything about the train conductor is shallow, petty, and false. His very insignificance is used to bring out more sharply Antonia's heroic nature. Even her misdirected loyalty reveals her strong, loving nature. Moreover, the hardships endured in consequence of Donovan's perfidy merely make manifest even further the noble qualities of her indomitable spirit. The fact is that the train man is treated throughout as a minor nuisance that can momentarily daunt but not destroy this vital personality who typifies all that is creative or life-giving, who is, in truth, a natural-born mother.

Yet a few suggestions may be advanced as to why Antonia did choose this particular worthless figure as love object. Allowing for the possibility that an infatuation can be irrational, we may note certain facts. First of all, the two men whom she always idolized were her father and Jim. Fastidious types both, they were certainly refined. Moreover, Grandmother Burden and Mrs. Harling combined to wrench Antonia away from rough farmers and the uncouth Ambrosch so that she might learn "nice ways". With such formulative influences she would be likely to look for a man with a cultivated manner. In addition, both her father and Jim were not hard-driving, aggressive individuals. Her sad father committed suicide. Jim walks his solitary way and is, to her way of thinking, largely un-appreciated. After graduation she makes a point of stopping to tell the boy's grandfather how splendid his speech was; and, according to Lena, she is always bragging about him and his prospects while he is away at school. Yet Jim, it is clear, is not hers to marry. Where will she find another "refined" young admirer? The Black Hawk boys with any education and community standing simply do not wed immigrant farm girls. Then along comes Donovan.

Willa Cather is famous for her economical style that wastes no words on unimportant facts or unnecessary details. Hence the details actually given are likely to be significant ones. We have seen that relatively little information is supplied about Donovan. Yet we are told that he makes a point of changing his clothes as soon as he leaves the train. Considering the dusty atmosphere of old-fashioned rail coaches - Jim himself talks of being "sticky and grimy" on one - Donovan would seem to be careful about his appearance. Secondly, he adopts a "dignified" and "aloof" air. Mr. Shimerda certainly had dignity, and Jim, one of the Burdens from Virginia, always is somewhat reserved. Finally, Donovan claims that he has failed to receive important railroad posts, for which he is qualified because "rough shod" men have been preferred. Here, too, Antonia would be reminded of her gentle, ineffectual father and Jim who had yet to make his mark.

One final aspect may be noted. Although Antonia has as an ideal a refined, gentlemanly type like her father or Jim, she seems at times curiously humble. Her mother, after all, was a peasant who married above her station in the Old Country, and Antonia tends to be grateful for kind words from the elite. After her return home, when Jim tells her that he has thought of her often, she asks tearfully, "How can it be like that, when you know so many people, and when I've disappointed you so?" They are longtime friends. She has him in mind frequently, but is amazed that he should think of her. Her attitude toward Donovan seems similar. Before she leaves, she worries lest in the city she will not be able to "manage so well for him". Upon her return, she admits that she never pressed him to marry her, hoping that if he saw how well she could "do for him," he would want to stay with her. If she was in love with him, it would seem that this was an almost servile devotion roused through superficial resemblances between him and the two men of whom she had long been genuinely fond. Interestingly enough, when she does marry, she chooses no "rough shod" man, but a former Viennese furrier who likes "theatres and lighted streets and music."

Also in this section, Jim notes with delight the progress made by the farm families since he first arrived in Nebraska as a small boy. The land, enriched and mellowed by the changing seasons, has become increasingly productive as a result of sustained human effort. Man, working in harmony with Nature, achieves deep satisfactions. Both adults and children, thinks Jim, are fortunate when this cooperative enterprise, giving rise to "sweeping lines of fertility." restores beauty and harmony to the world.

Antonia, the "natural-born mother," is clearly in this picture. Donovan is just the opposite. He takes and does not give. He is all that is shabby, mean, and essentially destructive. Yet while he can cause Antonia grief, she is too much in harmony with all that is life-giving or creative in the land to be permanently wrecked. Her spirit is strong and unquenchable. Incidentally, here again the town is contrasted with the country. Larry takes Antonia away from the farmland she loves to the city. There life is hard for her, and she finds that even her clothes cannot be cleaned properly. Is the literal dirt used to signify other less clean aspects of urban life? She returns, and her clothes are washed and dried in the sun. From the earth Antonia draws the strength to accept her disappointments and go on, like the other productive farm people, to contribute to the country's progress.

The last point to be considered is Miss Cather's use of the Widow Steavens as narrator for the story of Antonia's sad affair. The rich vernacular speech of this spry, spirited older woman is pleasant in itself, and the character is beautifully drawn. This also permits the novelist to handle the recital with both sympathy and reticence. The Widow, after all, will not be expected to know everything about the relationship, and Jim will not be one to pry. This way we are given the bare facts of the situation, permitted briefly to cry "like a young one" over Antonia's misfortune, and then briskly encouraged to observe that since then, and despite difficulties the girl has "got on fine."

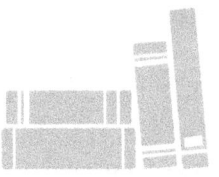

MY ANTONIA

TEXTUAL ANALYSIS

BOOK V: CUZAK'S BOYS

....

Not for twenty years does Jim keeps his promise to come back to Antonia. He knows that she married a young Bohemian cousin of Anton Jelinek. He has heard, too, that they had many children and for years were not prosperous because her husband lacked force. Jim once sent her pictures of her native village from abroad, but has hitherto avoided visits for fear of finding her old and worn. He prizes his early memories and wants no more illusions shattered.

Eventually, however, he receives happier reports from Lena and Tiny and decides to stop over in Nebraska. According to Lena, Anton Cuzak, whom Antonia married, is not a hard-driving type, but she is fond of him and proud of their ten or eleven children.

Approaching the Cuzak farm, Jim meets three small boys, one of whom looks full of mischief. Two older girls in the kitchen greet him politely and seek their mother. Strong, sunburned, somewhat grayed, Antonia has the same unforgettable eyes. Still, vigorous, she seems "battered but not diminished." After failing at first to recognize him, she receives him with all the old warmth and introduces her children. Their father is with the oldest boy at a street fair in Wilbur. She is distressed to learn that Jim has no children.

Jim is later taken to view the new fruit cave, near the house. As the youngsters afterwards race out into the sun, Jim sees then as an "explosion of life out of the dark cave." He then is shown the flourishing groves and orchards, as well as a charming grape arbor, all of which Antonia has lovingly tended. The early years were difficult, she admits, because her husband became easily discouraged. She worked hard, however, and later the children helped. Her first baby, Martha, is now married and has a son. She loves the farm, but does not regret having learned "nice ways" at the Harlings. She will never, however, send her daughters out to be hired girls, nor will she have to.

That evening, Jim is shown family pictures, and Leo the impish boy who is Antonia's favorite, plays old Mr. Shimerda's violin. The next day, Cuzak returns, a short, rumpled man with a black curly mustache. He and young Rudolph tell of the fair. Later the lad recounts how Wick Cutter finally shot his wife and then committed suicide, making sure that having survived her even briefly he could still dispose of his wealth. Cuzak also tells Jim about his early life in Europe. He misses the bright lights but loves and admires Antonia. Jim leaves, and spends a disappointing day in Black Hawk. Walking out into the country, he remembers the early days and thinks how Destiny shaped the lives of Antonia and the boy Jim. He will now see more of her and her family, for she shares with him the precious past.

CHARACTER ANALYSIS: BOOK V

Jim Burden

In this section, Jim's reluctance to risk any clouding of his bright image of Antonia as strong and indomitable is brought out. As a successful lawyer and an old friend, he might have come to offer some assistance when he heard that she was poor and had a large family. Willa Cather herself made every effort to send thoughtful gifts of money or sometimes even seed to old Nebraska farm friends when times were hard. Jim, however, mails some pictures from Bohemia, but stays away lest he see Antonia "aged and broken." Only when Lena gives him a "cheerful" account of Antonia's situation does he finally get up the courage to pay a call.

Meeting her again, he is deeply moved. As he feared, she does look older after twenty years of intense effort, but as a personality she still has undiminished vigor. This he finds reassuring. She has, of course, lost teeth, but he is consoled to discover that she has retained the "fire of life." Meeting all her well-mannered, handsome children and admiring her neat house and flourishing farm, Jim is much affected. Watching the young people streak out of the dark cave, he feels for the moment dizzy.

He is particularly taken with the older sons. They make him feel like a boy again, and he finds long-forgotten interests revived in him. He tells them that he was once very much in love with their mother. As he lies down to sleep with the boys, he is again aware of the vivid images Antonia has always left in his mind. She represents timeless and universal human attitudes and stimulates the imagination. She makes one feel the meaning of ordinary happenings, the wonders of making things grow. Generous in every way, she is to Jim a "rich mine of life." From this it can be seen that Jim still values her more as a symbol than as a person. Her image, "strengthened and simplified," as were those of Otto and Russian Peter when he read the classics in Lincoln, has been one of the sustaining forces of his life. Fortunately, when he at last dares to return, he finds that she is still the great spirit he had envisioned over the years.

Cuzak he regards as interesting and companionable. His description of "Papa" as a "crumpled little man" with a quaint habit of looking at one sidewise, after the manner of a workhorse, seems tinged with condescension. Yet he likes talking to him about Vienna and the gay city life that the Bohemian so misses. He looks forward to taking the boys on camping trips and enjoying long walks in the future with Cuzak. If his reactions to Antonia are those of a man who depends much upon idealized memories and inspiring symbols, his response to the hospitable men of the family suggests that here is a lonely, childless individual ready to adopt a whole ready-made family.

Finally, there is still in Jim the vaguely mystical strain evident in the earlier chapters. Returning to the countryside near Black Hawk, he again feels the sensation of being obliterated. Once again, too, he is conscious of the force of destiny and more aware than ever how much his first childhood years exploring the prairie with Antonia have meant to him as a man.

Antonia Shimerda Cuzak

When Jim meets her again, Antonia is pleased and excited. As she asks him to stay to meet her husband and her oldest son, she is "panting with excitement." Obviously, Antonia has remained capable of enthusiasm. She is, in fact, so "stirred up," she can hardly talk. She goes on to say that she feels as young as ever and can do as much work. She is happy and very pleased with her family and her home. She jokes about her fondness for the prankish Leo and soothes the tearful little boy whose dog has just died. She talks with awed satisfaction of all the bread she has to bake and confesses that she loves her trees as if they were people. She thanks God for her good health and calmly declares that had it not been for her strength they would never have been able to keep the farm going during the hard years when Cuzak was ready to give up. She herself has never been discouraged and never lonely. Life may have been easier in town, but while there she used to be confused and ill at ease. Here she works unceasingly, but is never sad. She evidently runs a good home. The children are happy and healthy, and the older ones help the younger. She encourages Leo to play his grandfather's violin, and she tells them all stories of the old days. She is fond of her husband and delighted to have him enjoy such little excursions as the one to the street fair. As for herself, she is a wonderfully contented wife and mother who has had all her own dreams come true and now labors cheerfully to give her many children the best possible chances.

Anton Cuzak

A good-humored, philosophical man, Cuzak is kindly and intelligent. He too enjoys life. His glowing description of the acrobats and dancing bear at the Fair reveals his capacity for experiencing joy. He is also considerate. Polite enough to substitute English for Bohemian since Jim is their guest, he cannot wait to tell Antonia about those who sent greetings to her from town. He also presents his gift of a paper snake gently to little Jan so as not to frighten the shy child. He is proud of his large family. He likes his children and seems to find them amusing. He misses the joys of city life, but has stayed on the farm and worked hard because of Antonia. She is so warm-hearted that he has been able to survive the isolation. Now he has his sons as companions. By no means so forceful as Antonia, Cuzak is not an unworthy husband for her. He seems to be bright, fairly cultivated, gentle, and hard-working. He may not be Mr. Shimerda or Jim, but neither is he a plodding farm hand.

Leo Cuzak

Antonia's favorite child, twelve-year-old Leo, is an independent, saucy young rascal. Curly-headed and handsome, he insists that his mother tell Jim that he was born on Easter Day. When she forgets, he butts her with his head. He is given to occasional scornful remarks and reminds Jim sometimes of the skeptical Mrs. Shimerda. He plays the violin fairly well for a self-taught boy, and seems both deeply sensitive and unusually daring. He appears to enjoy things more than other people and hates to make deliberate judgments. When Jim leaves, Leo runs off without saying good-bye. He may have been sorry to see Jim go, or he may have been jealous because Antonia showed the visitor so much attention. No one knows, says his older brother, Ambrosch.

Wick Cutter

As an old man, Wick looks like a dried-up little monkey but still quarrels unceasingly with his palsied wife. More and more he becomes obsessed with the dread that she will inherit from him, since under the law a surviving wife can at least claim one-third. So he buys a pistol ostensibly to shoot a cat, and one night when there are many within earshot kills his wife. He then shoots himself, but times his shot so that he is alive after she is and can tell this to the horrified men who rush into the house. Antonia is amazed that anyone could have such a cold heart. Wick to the end, however, shows a perverse kind of mental alertness and courage, as well as a macabre sense of humor. Although his actions are dreadful, he still seems an oddly comic creation.

Comment: Book V

Anton Cuzak is based on a young Bohemian named Pavelka, who married the original Annie Sadilek. He also suggested the hero for Miss Cather's famous short story "Neighbor Rosicky" and was quite proud of the honor (Bennett, 50). The Pavelkas, like the Cuzaks in the story, had a great many children. Whenever she returned on visits to Nebraska, the novelist enjoyed going out to see them on their farm. She was particularly impressed with the good manners of the young people. Incidentally, she, too, sent her Bohemian friend pictures from Czechoslovakia, which the family continued to cherish (Bennett, 49-53).

The bizarre deaths of Wick Cutter and his wife also are based upon actual happenings. M. R. Bentley, the original Red Cloud money-lender, did kill his wife and himself in this manner. The only striking difference in the fictional accounts is that Wick leaves only a relatively small estate, whereas Bentley's was considerably greater (Bennett, 84-5). Again, however, the author intends to make a point. Cutter, the mean, avaricious individual, shrivels physically and dies wretchedly to deprive his wife of a rather insignificant sum. Antonia, warm and generous, who was once his intended victim, lives on to be happy and prosperous.

In many of her stories Willa Cather depicts heroines who are stronger and abler than their men. It is clear that Cuzak is by no means a contemptible figure. He is intelligent, good-natured, affectionate, and hard-working. Yet there can be little doubt as to who runs things on the Cuzak farm. Antonia is clearly the more dynamic, the more vigorous of the two. She says flatly that had it not been for her physical hardihood they could never have kept the farm going during the difficult early years. It was she also who, after her husband was asleep, went down to water the young trees that eventually formed the beautiful orchards that Jim admires. Far from denying her claim, Cuzak readily admits that he would have given up long ago had it not been for his warmhearted, determined wife. Jim describes Cuzak graphically as the "instrument" of Antonia's life mission.

Interestingly enough, there is no indication that Jim envies Cuzak. He seems, in fact, to be almost sorry for the little man. Although Jim's admiration for Antonia as the symbol of motherhood at its best may be almost boundless, he sees at once that the lot of her devoted husband may be far from ideal. His first impression of Cuzak is of a "humorous philosopher who had hitched up one shoulder under the burdens of life." He notes that the Cuzaks are on the friendliest of terms but sees Anton as the "corrective" and his wife as the main "impulse." Cuzak's own words have a wistful quality. He guesses that Antonia was right to keep them on the farm. He is grateful that she is not too strict with him, allowing him occasionally an extra beer in town. All in all, she is "a good wife for a poor man." Yet he does miss the sociable evenings in the city. This is particularly interesting when we recall how desperately homesick Mr. Shimerda was for his old cronies who used to talk with him "about music, and the woods, and about God." The dilemma is clear. Antonia wanted a husband as much as possible like her father and Jim. Yet neither of these men ever wanted to live permanently far from urban life. When she found a man who met her standards, he did not really want an isolated farm existence either. Love for her and for their children has kept him out in the country for over twenty years, but his mildly regretful tone causes Jim to wonder if the life that is desirable for one is ever perfect for another. Jim himself has had his difficulties with an energetic, executive wife. Here he seems almost to join forces with Cuzak. Both, being cosmopolitan in spirit, can talk of Vienna together.

The point has been made previously that *My Antonia* is to a great extent autobiographical. The underlying question posed at the end seems to be one that Miss Cather herself had to answer. The more she saw of urban life in the America of her time, the more she came to dislike it. This attitude is particularly apparent in such novels as *One of Ours* and *The Professor's House*. Life there was meanly materialistic and small-minded, in contrast with the happy creative home life of a Burden or Cuzak farm. Yet from the first, she herself was attracted by the richer cultural opportunities offered in the great cities. She liked the theatre and the concert hall. She enjoyed talking with cultivated people. She also took pleasure in visiting other lands. Although discouraging distracting intrusions upon her privacy, she delighted in entertaining close friends and serving them delicacies and fine wines. All that Mr. Shimerda and poor Cuzak longed for, she too would have sadly missed. Yet she still maintained that a life close to nature, such as that developed by Antonia, was ideally the most rewarding. In the marriage of Antonia and Cuzak, the two modes of existence are merged. Yet Miss Cather cannot honestly report that the situation equally satisfies both parties. She herself settled for the city, but went off to a remote resort or the sparsely populated Southwest or back to visit Nebraska whenever she felt the need for a spiritual tonic.

The use of symbols is particularly noteworthy in this final section. Antonia's secluded grape arbor with its benches for repose seems to sum up fittingly the serene, orderly, fruitful life that Jim's friend has worked out for herself. The old Shimerda violin, played by Leo, along with the carefully described photographs of former friends, suggests Antonia's resolve to pass on cherished traditions to her descendants. Above all, the striking picture of the children racing up from the dark cave into the sunlight is significant. On the one hand, it represents the good things growing out of the farm's dark soil. On the other, it calls to mind the wretched conditions in the gloomy Shimerda cave during the first bitter winter. These healthy, laughing young people are Shimerda grandchildren.

As the story ends, Jim, who is childless, seems to plan to treat the Cuzak boys almost as foster sons. Antonia in the past has often been kind to him. Is she now about to provide him with some of the needed satisfactions of a solid, family life? For that matter is this what in a limited way old friends like the Pavelkas did for Willa Cather?

As Jim sees life after all his extensive travels, the small town is depressing and the city cold. Here, however, among these country people, with their strength and warmth, good humor and unflagging enthusiasm, he feels at last at home. With his cosmopolitan experience, he brings the great world to their small farm, and this they welcome. They, in turn, give him a reassuring sense that life can have rich positive values which produce peace and contentment.

In the last chapter there is an artistic rounding out of the work, with three **themes** re-introduced that were sounded at the beginning of the story. First of all, there is the golden beauty of the prairie in autumn that rouses a feeling of exaltation.

Secondly, there is the awesome idea of being so absorbed into the vastness of nature as to feel obliterated or blotted out. Finally, there is the concept of destiny as a great mysterious force that determines the course of lives. Whatever difficulties and disappointments this fate originally ordained for Jim and Antonia, it at least made it possible for them as children to share a succession of wonderful adventures. Such stimulating experiences later sustained them individually and established between them an imperishable bond.

Although many lively incidents are vividly described in *My Antonia*, the **episodes** are related not so much for their intrinsic interest as for the effect they have upon those participating. This is essentially a psychological novel about two highly impressionable people temperamentally capable of enthusiasm. Its main appeal will probably always be to readers who feel strongly about things and go on regarding life as a great adventure to be enjoyed to the hilt.

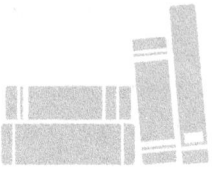

MY ANTONIA

CHARACTER ANALYSES

In Willa Cather's novels the good, or admirable characters often reveal the same basic traits, and the less agreeable figures, too, also have certain qualities in common. The outline form has been used here to make this more apparent. It is also worth remarking, however, that even favorably drawn individuals are shown to have some faults, and that less noble ones are not always seen at their worst.

ANTONIA SHIMERDA

(1) is generous. She offers Jim her ring for teaching her some English, lavishly praises his killing of the snake, never spares herself when working for those she likes.

(2) is intelligent. She learns quickly, asks questions, and even as a girl has opinions on everything.

(3) is independent. She is not cowed by the strongminded Mr. Harling, and she does not hide away her first child.

(4) is courageous. She weathers well such disasters as her father's suicide and Donovan's treachery, and keeps up her husband's spirits during years of poor crops.

(5) is hard-working. She does a man's work in the fields and later energetically labors to build up the Cuzak place.

(6) is good to children. She is the loyal big sister to Jim, makes candy for the young Harlings, and is obviously a wonderful mother to her own big family.

(7) likes animals and plants. She tends the dying insect, gives up hunting, and cultivates a splendid garden.

(8) has respect for order. Her house is well run, with the older children trained to help the younger.

(9) has respect for tradition. She remembers fondly stories of her father and of Jim and passes them on.

(10) has a feeling for beauty. She likes music and dancing, draws inspiration and solace from the land, and creates a lovely, peaceful garden.

Negatively she also

(11) can be foolhardy. She is unwise to go to work for Wick Cutter.

(12) can be unreasonably loyal. She will not listen to friends who distrust Donovan.

JIM BURDEN

(1) is generous. He offers his scarf to Yulka, gives up the dances to please his grandmother, rejoices in Antonia's prosperity.

(2) is intelligent. He recognizes early the fine qualities of Mr. Shimerda and rejects the narrow views of many in Black Hawk.

(3) is independent. He ignores the snobbish younger set and chooses the country girls as friends.

(4) is courageous. He does kill the snake and fight Cutter, and he refuses to conform with Black Hawk prejudices.

(5) is hard-working. He studies much alone when preparing for the University, taking off only the day of the picnic.

(6) has respect for tradition. Like Antonia, he treasures the memory of Mr. Shimerda.

(7) has a feeling for beauty. He describes often his joy in the changing splendors of the Nebraska landscape.

Negatively, he also

(8) can judge harshly. He dislikes foreigners after Jake's fight with Ambrosch, and is angry when Antonia lets herself be deceived by Larry.

(9) can act selfishly. He leaves Lena rather abruptly and stays away for twenty years lest he be dismayed at finding Antonia no longer triumphant.

GRANDFATHER BURDEN

(1) is generous. He is good to Jim and helps the Shimerdas even when they seem mean and ungrateful.

(2) is intelligent. Although convinced that his type of religion and his way of living are good, he can appreciate the views of the manly Jelinek and the Catholic piety of a Mr. Shimerda.

(3) is hard-working. Although aging, he labors with the hired men.

Negatively, he also

(4) can be narrow-minded. Even Grandmother worries about his strong views on religion, and he keeps Jelinek away from Jim, although the Bohemian's saloon is respectable.

GRANDMOTHER BURDEN

(1) is generous. She is kind to Jim and to Antonia, and even to the disagreeable Mrs. Shimerda. She also lets the horse be sacrificed when help must be obtained.

(2) is intelligent. Even when her patience is strained, she sees something in the Shimerda viewpoint.

(3) is courageous. She fights snakes with her cane and braves Mrs. Shimerda's ire to keep Yulka from being frightened at the burial service.

(4) likes animals. She will not let the badger be killed.

(5) has a feeling for order and beauty. Her house is clean and attractive, and she works hard to keep it so.

Negatively, she also

(6) can be narrow-minded. She is impatient with the sorely beset Shimerdas and won't try their unfamiliar mushrooms. She also stops Jim from going to the dances attended by the country girls and their friends.

MR. SHIMERDA

(1) is generous. He marries his wife to protect her good name, gives up his friends for her and the children, and hopes to give Jim his prized gun.

(2) is intelligent. He has read much and always delighted in amicable discussions.

(3) has a feeling for order and beauty. He hates the dark, depressing Shimerda cave and appreciates the Burdens' hospitality. He is also a musician.

Negatively, he also

(4) lacks force. Although he knows more, he cannot handle his wife and Ambrosch.

(5) lacks stamina. He gives in to despair and kills himself.

MRS. HARLING

(1) is generous. She is good to Antonia and Jim, even forgiving them for having strongly opposed her.

(2) is intelligent. Note how quickly she takes the measure of Ambrosch and Mrs. Shimerda, and also of Donovan.

(3) is hard-working. She attacks domestic chores vigorously.

(4) has respect for order. Her household is well conducted.

(5) has a feeling for beauty. She likes music and can appreciate Antonia's enjoyment of good threshing weather.

Negatively, she also

(6) has a fiery temper. She is furious when defied.

LENA LINGARD

(1) is generous. She is kind to her little brother and builds her mother a house. She lets Jim go gracefully and sends wedding gifts to Antonia, who tried to keep Jim away from her.

(2) is intelligent. She runs her business and her life efficiently. She learns all that she needs to know for success.

(3) is independent. She leaves town to start her own business, rejects offers of marriage to stay free, and pays her own way.

(4) has a feeling for beauty. She creates good-looking clothes and enjoys the theatre. She likes to dance.

(5) shows warm sympathy for people. She acts understandingly toward Ole Benson, the Colonel, and Ordinsky, as well as Jim. She even suffers with characters in plays.

Negatively, she also

(6) falls short of Antonia's selflessness. She enjoys the attentions of male admirers but wants none of the responsibilities of marriage.

ANTON CUZAK

(1) is generous. He gives his wife full credit for their prosperity, is hospitable to Jim, and brings home gifts to his children.

(2) is intelligent. He takes an interest in Jim's travels and asks interesting questions.

(3) is hard-working. He may sometimes have become discouraged but he struggled along with Antonia to make the farm pay.

(4) has artistic interests. He speaks of opera singers and Vienna and misses the cultural advantages of the city.

Negatively, he also

(5) seems less forceful than his wife. During the hard years he lost heart, but she never faltered.

MRS. SHIMERDA

(1) is mean-spirited. She whines and complains, envies the Burdens, and resents their generosity.

(2) is greedy. She snatches Mrs. Burden's iron pot and is unwilling to pay fully for the cow.

(3) is stupid. Despite a certain shrewdness, or cunning, she does not plan efficiently or run her home well.

Positively, she also

(4) has some initiative. She insisted that the family emigrate.

(5) has force and stamina. She does not collapse after her husband's death, but goads her children on to work, and labors along with them.

AMBROSCH SHIMERDA

(1) is mean-spirited. He has a surly manner, ruins the harness and will not admit it, works his sister hard, sneers at Antonia's baby, and drives off the Widow Steavens.

(2) is greedy. He tries to get his hands on most of Antonia's wages but is prevented by Mrs. Harling.

(3) is disagreeable. He has none of the social graces.

Positively, he also

(4) is hard-working. He is never shown to be lazy.

(5) is pious. He prays for his father and has Masses said.

(6) gives Antonia a fair dowry. He also at least takes her in again when she returns home in disgrace:

WICK CUTTER

(1) is mean-spirited. He takes unfair advantage of immigrant farmers with limited resources and little knowledge of mortgage regulations.

(2) is greedy. He cheats many farmers and does not even want to leave his wife or her family any of his money when he dies. So he kills her and then himself.

(3) is sensually corrupt. He seduces two hired girls and plans to add Antonia to his victims but is prevented by Jim.

(4) is hypocritical. He mouths moral maxims and ostentatiously contributes to the church.

(5) is clever. He taxes the best efforts of Frances Harling and Grandfather Burden to extricate the farmers from his clutches. His scheme to surprise Antonia is ingenious, and his final gruesome jest at least shows planning.

(6) is almost perversely good-humored. He enjoys his wife's taking orders for painted china, cheerfully puts her on the wrong train, and even dies with a comic flourish.

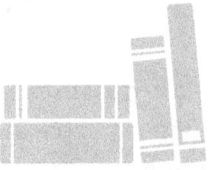

MY ANTONIA

CRITICAL COMMENTARY

OVER-ALL ESTIMATE

Over the years the general critical reaction to *My Antonia* has been favorable. This is the fourth of Willa Cather's twelve novels and appeared in 1918 when she was in her mid-forties. By then, having served her apprenticeship, she had developed her characteristic style. Her view of life had matured, and her material, taken from the happiest period of her youth in Nebraska, was such that she could handle it with discernment and deep feeling.

AUTOBIOGRAPHICAL MATERIAL

My Antonia grew out of vivid recollections of old friends and exciting childhood experiences. Mildred R. Bennett, in *The World of Willa Cather*, interestingly identifies the original Nebraskans on whom characters were based. She tells of Miss Cather's grandparents who became the elder Burdens, of the Sadileks who suggested the Shimerdas, and of the Red Cloud residents who served as models for the Harlings, the Cutters, and the

Gardeners. She also gives information about Miss Cather's family, pioneer life in Nebraska, and the State University which the novelist (and Jim) attended.

Other background material is supplied by two of Miss Cather's close friends. Elizabeth Shepley Sergeant, in *Willa Cather: A Memoir*, says that during the period when *My Antonia* was written, the author "lived and swam in the high seas of memory." When planning the book, Miss Cather told Miss Sergeant that she wanted to display her heroine as one would an attractive object placed in the middle of a table, that people could look at and admire from all sides. She later declared that *My Antonia* in effect "wrote itself."

In *Willa Cather Living*, Edith Lewis, who for years shared the author's home, notes how revolutionary the book seemed when it was published. It had no conventional plot and no love story, and some readers were disappointed that it gave so much prominence to mere hired girls. The initial sale was small. The author made only $1300 the first year, says Miss Lewis, and $400 the next.

SUPERIOR STYLE

Later commentators have spoken highly of the novel's artistry. Maxwell Geismar, for instance, sees its craftsmanship as superior to that of the earlier *O Pioneers!* He finds the descriptions of the frontier more "graceful," the characterizations sharper, and the **episodes** more vividly recounted. He lauds, too, her recognition of the plight of uprooted immigrants and her shrewd evaluation of the social situation in Black Hawk. Francis X. Connolly calls it one of her "crucial" books because it marks new progress in her emergence as a symbolic writer.

THE PROBLEM OF THE NARRATOR

Nevertheless, one question about the work's form is sometimes raised. Some have voiced dissatisfaction with the use of Jim Burden as narrator. E. K. Brown, author of the standard critical biography, believes that problems exist because Jim must serve two different purposes. He must be at once both the friend and admirer of Antonia, and a detached, impartial observer. David Daiches, too, takes up the issue in his work *Willa Cather: A Critical Introduction.* He notes that having someone tell the story in the first person is in accord with the autobiographical element in the work, but thinks that the device also has its perils. No mere observer can know everything about a girl like Antonia. Hence she sometimes seems less important as a person than as a symbol stimulating strong emotions in the narrator. He believes that Miss Cather never wholly overcame this difficulty. John H. Randall, in his stimulating recent study, *The Landscape and the Looking Glass*, takes a different stand. He does not see Jim as merely a narrator. He holds that Jim's story is almost as important as Antonia's. The two characters have life histories that are parallel but contrasting, with Antonia and Jim representing youth and age, heart and head, actor and spectator, success and failure.

NOSTALGIC TONE

Most critics also make some comment upon the melancholy mood of the novel. The opening pages establish, of course, that the narrative will embody the precious childhood memories of a disappointed man. The very fact that those "best days" have long since flown, will account for reflections tinged with nostalgia. Yet E. K. Brown suggests that herein lies the key to the book as a whole. It is intended mainly to "convey a feeling," the emotion being a "mournful appreciation" of great adventures gone by.

For his part, Lionel Trilling links this element of sadness with Willa Cather's profound awareness of the inevitable doom of all pioneers. To realize their dreams, new settlers had to face the most severe of hardships. Some would fail, but even those who succeeded would lose some greatness in a world of material comforts that no longer challenged the spirit. By the time that Antonia is in her twenties, the frontier civilization has begun to decline. All that she, or any great-souled individual, can do under such circumstances is to make the best of things. To Alfred Kazin, Willa Cather's *My Antonia* is the "best and purest of her elegies." He too finds that her heroine's most significant achievement lies simply in "a rigid determination to see one's life through." Randall, on the other hand, concentrates upon the final pleasant scenes of fulfillment and contentment which Jim encounters on Antonia's farm. Antonia here is a veritable goddess presiding over "the garden of the world" and combining the "vitality of nature" with the order derived from civilization. He thus finds this the "most affirmative," or generally hopeful, book that the novelist ever wrote.

SPIRITUAL THEME

Most commentators thus have theories as to the work's main theme. Randall, as indicated above, sees *My Antonia* as an "agrarian idyll," a story glorifying country life at its best, with man living in harmony with nature. Daiches, on the other hand, declares that the central factor is the "development and self-discovery of the heroine." In their recent and thought-provoking study, *Willa Cather's Gift of Sympathy*, Edward A. and Lillian D. Bloom hold that here, as elsewhere, the novelist's primary interest is in man's spiritual quest. The pioneers stand for all human beings striving to attain an ideal and attempting to find a sanctuary of some permanence. In *My Antonia*, the land itself is that sought-for sanctuary, but only to those who, like the generous Bohemian girl, pay proper homage to Nature. Finally, there is the view of Alfred Kazin that also takes into account Willa Cather's passionate idealism. The great **theme** of all her novels, he declares, is the "struggle between grandeur and meanness, the two poles of her world."

MY ANTONIA

REVIEW QUESTIONS AND ANSWERS

Question: The heroism of Miss Cather's pioneers consists in surviving hardships and overcoming obstacles. Indicate the different types of difficulties encountered by the immigrants in *My Antonia*.

Answer: First of all, there is the language barrier. Unable to communicate, the newly arrived Shimerdas cannot ask for needed help, make friends easily, or avoid relying upon a scoundrel like Krajiek. Second, there is the rigorous Nebraska climate. Were the winter less severe, Mr. Shimerda and his sons might have been able to escape the prolonged unpleasantness of life in the cave and to arrange for a more adequate food supply. Third, there is the lack of cooperation among the immigrants themselves. Krajiek, already well established, wants only to cheat his countrymen. Otto, the Austrian, distrusts the Czechs, and the Norwegians refuse to permit the burial of Mr. Shimerda in their cemetery. Fourth, there is prejudice on the part of the native-born Americans. Even the kindly and tolerant Burdens find some of the older European customs hard to tolerate, and the Black Hawk snobs regard all foreigners as inferiors. Finally, some problems stem from individual personality traits. Mr.

Shimerda's painful loneliness, his wife's whining manner and general inefficiency, Ambrosch's sullen rudeness, and even poor Russian Peter's shyness, all help to worsen the plight of those already at a severe disadvantage. Many, however, do go on to achieve an eventual solid prosperity. And their struggle, to Miss Cather, is the measure of their greatness.

Question: What part does Antonia's European background play in the formation of her strong, creative personality?

Answer: Arriving in America as a girl of fourteen, Antonia has already acquired excellent values from the gentle, cultivated father she so passionately admires. At home he was a violinist who delighted in the company of fellow musicians. He also read many books and liked to talk over stimulating ideas with old friends in a pleasant garden setting. From him she undoubtedly obtained her feeling for music and her eagerness to learn. His whole nature is noble and generous. He married her mother only because he thought it the honorable thing to do, and he suffers greatly when he must accept charity from the Burdens. He understands, too, Antonia's warm-hearted urge to keep life in the frail insect. Affectionate to her, courteous to all, he suggests always that same greatness of spirit that later distinguishes her from the petty snobs of Black Hawk. From her mother, on the other hand, Antonia doubtless derives her rugged constitution. Mrs. Shimerda may be somewhat incompetent and often disagreeable, but she is determined and does survive the worst of winters. To make her way in the world and wrest victory from the soil, Antonia would have to be far stronger than the listless town girls. Actually she has both her mother's peasant toughness and her father's vision, but none of the older residents cramping prejudices. Thus she can put in years of incredibly hard physical effort and eventually achieve the good life originally outlined for her by her Old World father. The secluded Cuzak garden would have charmed him, and his grandson now plays his beloved violin.

Question: In *My Antonia* does the author idealize all European immigrants at the expense of native-born Nebraska settlers?

Answer: As in her other stories about immigrant pioneers, Willa Cather here does stress the admirable qualities of people from non-English-speaking lands. Her portrayal of Antonia, for instance, emphasizes the Bohemian girl's kindness, generosity, courage, perseverance, and amiable good nature. Lena and Tiny also possess commendable traits, as do the other hired girls, Russian Peter, the Austrian Otto, and, among the Bohemians, Mr. Shimerda, Anton Jelinek, and Anton Cuzak. By contrast the Black Hawk townspeople seem pale and dull, if not narrow-minded or snobbish. Young men like Harry Paine and Sylvester Lovett are regarded with contempt, and Wick Cutter is, of course, a scoundrel.

On the other hand, not all Europeans are noble, and not all native Americans base. Within the Shimerda group, the father is a suicide, the mother is meanly spiteful, Ambrosch is sullen, and Marek weakminded. Krajiek is greedy and unscrupulous, and the Norwegians are uncooperative at the time of the Shimerda funeral. Among the early settlers, the Burdens are kindly, tolerant, and generally helpful. The Harlings, too, are above reproach, and the Widow Steavens is a true friend in need. Others in the community also volunteer aid at the time of burial. Hence, while the heroine and certain other favorably drawn characters are Europeans, not all immigrants are represented as intellectually or morally superior to their neighbors born in this country.

Question: For much of his life Jim Burden lives far from Antonia and moves in circles far different from hers. Why has she meant so much to him?

Answer: Youth to Willa Cather is the period when deepest, most lasting impressions are formed. Jim meets Antonia when he is ten and she is four years older. They have both been uprooted from their birthplaces and set down in a wild new country. Everything to them is novel and exciting, and, except for little Yulka, there are no other children near. They therefore share uniquely the joys of exploration and discovery. In addition, they are together during such startling **episodes** as the killing of the snake and the deathbed horror tale of Pavel. Later in Black Hawk, Jim must share her with the Harlings, the hired girls, and various male escorts. Nevertheless, she still takes a strong interest in his welfare, and he, in turn, considers her the best dancer in town, typifying all that is vivacious and gay in the country girls.

From the first, Antonia, ever generous, gives the lonely boy the praise and encouragement he needs. She extols him to everyone for killing the snake. She urges him to study hard and insists that he will succeed. She also keeps him from becoming too friendly with Lena so that he will have the chance to forge ahead. Finally she is the daughter of Mr. Shimerda, of whom he thought a great deal. She is thus, in a sense, his link with the rich culture of the Old World, which her father represented. Jim is therefore especially pleased at the end to find out that Antonia has kept faith magnificently with the noblest ideals for which the old violinist stood.

Question: Heroism is often represented in fiction in terms of individual spectacular feats. In *My Antonia* does this type of showy accomplishment receive major emphasis?

Answer: On at least two occasions Jim Burden is heroic in this conventional sense. He kills a rattlesnake, and he bests a midnight assailant in brutal hand-to-hand combat. In both instances, however, the nobler aspects of the boy's achievements are played down. The account of the snake **episode** brings out the element of blind chance, the boy's instinctive rather than deliberate action, the weakness and torpor of the old snake, the foolish vanity of the young victor, and the exaggerated praise of him by the loyal and generous Antonia. In the fight with Wick Cutter there is stress upon Jim's distaste for the role of gallant protector, his wild flight across town afterwards in his night clothes, his terror lest the town hear of the matter and laugh at him, and his fury at Antonia for getting him into it. In some ways Jim is a genuine romantic, but he is hardly the usual shining knight. In minor episodes, such as Jake's quarrel with Ambrosch, the treatment is no more serious. Far more impressive throughout is the heroism of determination and endurance represented by Antonia. Her father's death deprives her of schooling and plunges her into exhausting farm work, but she proudly takes on man-sized tasks without complaint. Later, when she returns home, unwed and abandoned, to bear her child, she feels keenly the shattering of her dreams and the scorn of the townsfolk. Once again, however, she accepts her hard lot, and prepares to make the best life possible for her baby. Finally, after she marries Cuzak, there are years of poor crops and small returns. Never daunted, she keeps up her husband's spirits and helps him build up a flourishing farm. This, to Willa Cather, is indeed heroism.

Question: Antonia marries a Bohemian immigrant, and her growing family speaks little English at home. Was she then virtually unaffected by her contacts as a girl with those born in this country?

Answer: Antonia as wife and mother may speak English rarely and prepare such Bohemian pastry treats as kolaches, but she has actually gained much from her friendships with Americans born here. Her mother was hardly the best of homemakers.

Grandmother Burden, by contrast, was capable and efficient. Antonia evidently learned much about the domestic arts from this wise old Virginia lady. She also acquired those refinements and graces of manner summed up in the expression "nice ways." Note how much cruder and rougher she seems when restricted for a time to the company of her mother and Ambrosch. Later, when she works for the Harlings, she becomes part of a well-run household in which there are several children. After her father's death, her life at home was grim and cheerless. Now she is a member of a happy family group. She has long known how to work; she learns at this how to play. At pleasant evening gatherings she is encouraged to tell stories, and she gladly makes candy and cookies. Moreover, the Harlings like music, and they introduce her to opera arias and plots. In town, too, she learns how to dance and how to dress, and subsequently the Widow Steavens helps her before and after she leaves with Donovan. Above all, she learns from Jim. He was her first teachers of English, and his respect for her father establishes a strong bond. Afterwards, as he goes on to college and law school and then travels extensively, he is her link with the great world beyond her farm. She is proud of all he has accomplished and talks of him admiringly to her children. Mrs. Cuzak is no copy of Mrs. Shimerda. Her sons, one feels, will go ahead, like Jim, to get the education she had to miss.

Question: After Antonia, Lena Lingard is the immigrant character whose history is related at the greatest length. What significant contributions does this character make to the novel as a whole?

Answer: The beautiful blonde Norwegian is, first of all, one of Jim's answers to those taking a contemptuous view of immigrant girls who work for a time as servants. Lena becomes a successful businesswoman among Americans and on strictly American terms. She is a talented dressmaker with creative ability. She works hard, learns to speak English well, and deals capably with employees and customers. There is also nothing crude or coarse about her. With her soft voice and gentle manner she attracts not only poor Ole Benson, or even the wild violinist, Ordinsky, but also the banker's son, Sylvester Lovett, the courtly Colonel Raleigh, and Jim himself. Remaining single, she does so strictly by choice.

Secondly, she has a special role to play in Jim's life. During his student days in Lincoln, she gives him the feminine companionship he needs. She is an attractive girl who can sob with him over Camille, prepare him a pleasant dinner, and give him news of home. She asks little in return, even paying her own way at the theatre, and lets him go gracefully when he must leave for Harvard. Her charm and sympathetic understanding have helped him mature. In love with her lightly and briefly, he learns for the first time what poetry is all about.

Finally, she serves as contrast to Antonia, who is even more selfless and generous. Lena builds a house for her mother, but has no wish to sacrifice herself for husband and children. Given the facts of her childhood poverty and misery, it is understandable that she values her personal freedom. Yet she obviously falls short, as does the wealthy Tiny, of Antonia's greatness of heart.

Question: *My Antonia* lacks a conventional plot. How does Willa Cather unify her varied material?

Answer: In the Introduction, Jim Burden declares that he has set down almost at random what he remembers of Antonia and the whole adventure of their childhood in Nebraska. We are thus warned not to expect a tightly knit plot. Yet his statement suggests three unifying factors. First of all, these are the memories of one man, Jim, already identified as a romantic personality. Most events will thus be seen from a single point of view and interpreted according to one person's standards or values. Secondly, there is Antonia herself. Although not present in all chapters, she is rarely altogether forgotten. Tiny Soderball's story, for instance, presents a kind of material success to be later contrasted with Antonia's deeper satisfactions; and Lena refers to her several times in the Lincoln scenes with Jim. Finally, the idea that the book will point up the "adventure" of early youth indicates a common element in such dissimilar experiences as the killing of the snake and the summertime picnic.

Two other devices, however, may also be considered. One is the use of minor characters as links. The Widow Steavens is mentioned several times in early sections although she will be important only when Antonia has her baby. Similar references are made to Larry Donovan and Anton Jelinek. On the other hand, Jake and Otto are recalled long after they have left the scene. Lastly, the progress of the seasons, so eloquently described, seems to carry the work along. The Nebraska landscape is essentially the same, but there is a kind of natural development as seed is planted and then crops are harvested, and as winter miseries yield to the hopefulness of spring.

Question: In *My Antonia* Willa Cather creates memorable scenes rich in such contrasting moods as sorrow and joy, hope and despair. Indicate how more than one emotion is suggested in several major episodes.

Answer: One of the most striking examples is the incident in which Antonia revives the failing insect. There is a chill in the air, and the girl herself is thinly clad. Yet her kind, affectionate nature seems briefly to restore life and hope. The insect's weak chirping in turn recalls memories of happy evenings in Europe when eager children gathered around the fire to hear

Old Hata. Those days, however have vanished, and with them Mr. Shimerda's hour of glory when he played at the weddings of noble benefactors.

Another such scene is that of the Christmas celebration. Thanks to the generous hired men, young Jim has a beautiful tree, with Otto's Austrian paper decorations adding a touch of enchantment.

Arriving for a visit, the sad Mr. Shimerda is warmly greeted and graciously entertained. A sociable man, he relaxes and for once seems almost cheerful. Nevertheless, all are aware that he must soon go out again into the bitter cold and that he will find the wretched Shimerda cave now more discouraging than ever.

The snake **episode** combines genuine terror with almost satiric humor as the shaken victor begins at once to strut with pride. Later at the Harling house, a sudden chill strikes during a pleasant social evening as Antonia tells of the tramp who killed himself at harvest time. On Commencement Day, Jim gives a good speech and is glad to be reconciled with Mrs. Harling. Yet afterwards he seems very much alone, and there is something wistful in the friendly tributes of the hired girls, who never had the chance to complete their schooling. Finally, the work as a whole consists of the happy memories of a man who went on to suffer many disappointments.

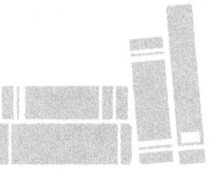

O PIONEERS!

PART I: THE WILD LAND

After eleven years of struggle, John Bergson, a Swedish immigrant, dies, leaving his family only their sod house and 640 acres of unyielding Nebraska prairie. His daughter, Alexandra, a strong, resolute blonde girl of twenty, rises to the challenge. She spurs on her stolid brothers, Lou and Oscar. She uses to advantage sound hints on hog-raising gleaned from Crazy Ivar, an eccentric but devout Russia hermit. When neighbors lose heart and give up their property, Alexandra persuades her reluctant brothers to make new purchases because in an exalted, almost mystical vision she foresees her land's bright future. She is saddened when Carl Linstrom, the sensitive, artistic boy she likes, leaves to live in Chicago. She then concentrates, however, upon advancing her youngest brother, Emil, for whom she has the highest hopes.

PART II: NEIGHBORING FIELDS

After sixteen years, the farm has prospered. Tall, handsome Emil, back from the University, becomes friendly with Marie, a vivacious, dark-haired Bohemian neighbor. She, however, is already married to Frank Shabbat, a moody, jealous young man. Lou and Oscar now have fussy, snobbish wives and several children. They vainly urge Alexandra, who has Ivar in her employ, to send the harmless old man off to an asylum. Carl returns, a far from wealthy engraver, now on route to Alaska. He remains for a month, and the older brothers warn Alexandra, now forty, against marrying him. They call him a fortune hunter and claim that she cannot morally present him with the farm their work made fruitful. Hurt and angry, she reminds them of her own part in the enterprise; but Carl, his pride wounded, leaves again. Meanwhile, Emil, attending a French Catholic fair, fitfully watches his friend Amedee dance happily with Angelique, his bride. Marie, for whom Emil longs, is not free. Restless, ill-at-ease, he goes off to Mexico City. Alexandra is alone.

PART III: WINTER MEMORIES

Alexandra hospitably welcomes Mrs. Lee, Lou's mother-in-law. She lets the old lady talk Swedish and wear her night-cap. Her guest is denied such privileges at home by a daughter who is ashamed of her foreign ways. Emil writes home vivid descriptions of Mexico, knowing that his sister will read them to Marie. Alexandra learns that the girl's married life brings her now only sorrow, but never links Marie with Emil. Actually, Emil to his sister remains the small boy with whom she shared such pleasant days as one when they beheld the beauty of a solitary white duck swimming in a small bay. Sometimes, however, she dreams of a strong, mysterious stranger carrying her off across the fields. At first this fancy angers her. In later years she finds it strangely soothing.

PARTY IV: THE WHITE MULBERRY TREE

Emil, in a dashing Mexican outfit, accompanies Alexandra to a French church supper. Amedee exults over the birth of his first son, and Marie tells fortunes. As a joke Amedee switches off the lights, and Emil kisses Marie for the first time. Startled, she tenderly responds. Days later, at the wedding of Signa, one of Alexandra's maids, Marie tells Emil that she cannot renounce her marriage vows and run off with him. He must leave, although she does love him. Within the month, Amedee dies suddenly of appendicitis. Their emotions stirred by this tragic event, Emil and Marie resolve to love unselfishly and part. Coming to say farewell, Emil finds her lying peacefully beneath a white mulberry. Overcome with desire, he makes love, and she yields. Her jealous husband, having drunk too much after the funeral, comes upon them and shoots to kill. Old Ivar discovers the bodies and staggers off horrified to tell Alexandra.

PART V: ALEXANDRA

The grieving Alexandra has heard nothing from Carl. Standing drenched at Emil's grave, she becomes ill and again dreams of being carried off by a strong man, whom she seems to recognize as Death. Because, however, she feels partially responsible for having brought the lovers together, she visits Frank in prison, promising the wretched man to work for his release. Carl returns, having just heard of the tragedy. He consoles her, and they plan at last to marry. They are old friends, not passionate young people, and she believes that they will find contentment. After a wedding trip to Alaska, they will return to the farm, for Carl knows that Alexandra belongs to the land.

Comment:

O Pioneers!, the first of Willa Cather's Nebraska novels, appeared in 1913. The title is from Walt Whitman's famous lyric, and the book is dedicated to Sarah Orne Jewett, the noted New England writer who had encouraged Miss Cather to write about the Western prairie country that she knew so well.

Alexandra, an early but characteristic Cather heroine, has the vision and the stamina to tame the "wild land" and make it productive. Her two brothers work hard and are physically robust; but they lack the imagination to try new methods, and they lose heart when crops for a time are poor. Growing older, they become narrowly conventional, pompous, and boastful. Alexandra, however, who loves the land and works in harmony with Nature, remains the great-souled individual, protecting the helpless like Old Ivar and running her household with dignity and grace.

Giving herself so completely to the land, Alexandra may still need companionship. Yet she will not become as passionately involved with another person as will Marie, Emil, and even Frank. She misses the intense joys of the young lovers, but she also is spared a measure of their agony. Alexandra is a strong, independent woman. She does experience fatigue, sadness, and loneliness, but years of determined effort and rigorous self-discipline have left her all but indomitable. Willa Cather sees such heroic pioneer women as typifying all that is solid, positive, and creative in American life.

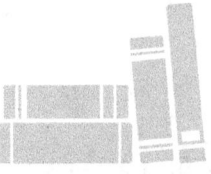

THE SONG OF THE LARK

PART I: FRIENDS OF CHILDHOOD

In Moonstone, a small Colorado town, around the year 1890, young Dr. Howard Archie pulls eleven-year-old Thea Kronborg through a dangerous attack of pneumonia. They become fast friends. Thea, the forthright blonde daughter of an unimpressive minister of Swedish descent, is encouraged to study music by her wise and capable mother. Her teacher is Professor Wunsch, a well trained Old World artist ruined by excessive drinking. He lives with the Kohlers, kindly German pair who take pride in their beautiful garden. Wunsch makes Thea work hard, astonished at her strong will and ability to apply herself.

Dr. Archie, unhappily married to a mean-spirited woman, likes to take Thea along on calls. With him she visits Spanish Johnny, a handsome, popular Mexican, who plays the mandolin and sings well. Sometimes, however, after an alcoholic spree he disappears for months, returning then sick and exhausted to his patient wife.

Another good friend is Ray Kennedy, a big, free-thinking, sentimental train conductor. Self-educated, always dreaming of fortunes in gold or oil, he hopes someday to marry Thea. He takes her with her brothers and Spanish Johnny to see the nearby Turquoise Hills, and tells her wonderful stories of the Southwest. That winter, Thea, now twelve, starts giving piano lessons and is allowed to have her own attic room. This she decorates with the help of her foolish but intensely loyal Aunt Tillie. Henceforth this room is her sanctuary.

A church Christmas concert proves disastrous for Thea when a snobbish woman, called Mrs. "Livery" Johnson because of her husband's business, secures every advantage for her mediocre rival, the insipid Lily Fisher. Thea, however, has started learning German from Wunsch, who knows she can sing movingly as well as play. Stifled in dull Moonstone, she tells Dr. Archie that she hopes someday to study abroad.

After a violent drinking bout, Wunsch leaves town, giving Thea his prized score of Orpheus. She takes over many of his pupils and gives up school. Mrs. Johnson criticizes her strictness with pupils, and her showily pious sister, Anna, rebukes her for playing waltzes on Sunday. Ray, however, takes her and her mother on a pleasant train excursion to Denver.

Thea is subsequently shaken by two grim events. A dirty tramp, harshly used by the town, kills himself in a way that poisons the water supply. Then a minor wreck fatally injures Ray. Gallantly considerate to the last, Ray has Dr. Archie see that his six-hundred-dollar insurance policy will give Thea her chance to study in Chicago. For the girl this is the start of a great adventure.

PART II: THE SONG OF THE LARK

Thea finds the city noisy and depressing, but works well with her teacher, Andor Harsanyi, a young, one-eyed Hungarian. She likes, too, visiting his gracious wife and children. Inviting her to sing one night after dinner, he is much impressed with her big natural voice, with its rich, full upper tones. After much thought he urges her to sing superbly rather than be a fair pianist. He sends her to Madison Bowers, a singing coach who is cold and greedy but who gives her excellent training.

Visiting Chicago's Art Institute, she admires a picture of a country girl called "The Song of the Lark." She also attends her first concert and finds the experience overwhelming. Returning for a visit at Moonstone, she enjoys an exhilarating musical evening singing with Spanish Johnny and the Mexicans. Her brothers and sisters, however, disapprove of her foreign friends, and she knows that she cannot stay longer at home. Dr. Archie reassures her that she will get what she really wants in time. He himself intends to make money in mining.

PART III: STUPID FACES

Back in Chicago, Thea earns her way by playing accompaniments for inept, easy going singers. She is lonely and restless until she meets Fred Ottenburg, a wealthy brewer whose hobby is music. He gets her a rewarding singing engagement at the home of the Nathanmeyers, a cultivated Jewish couple. Afterwards, when she seems ill and exhausted, Fred sends her to his Arizona ranch.

PART IV: THE ANCIENT PEOPLE

Thea relaxes happily at the ranch and finds new strength of purpose as she contemplates the nearby cliff-dwellings of ancient tribes. After two months Fred arrives and joins her for canyon picnic. She enjoys his attentions and agrees to go with him to Mexico. She believes that he means to marry her, but unknown to her he has a wife in California, from whom he has long been separated. He loves Thea but doubts that she wants permanent ties anyway.

PART V: DR. ARCHIE'S VENTURE

Summoned by Thea to New York, Dr. Archie, whose mining interests are prospering, sells some shares to lend her money for study abroad. Fred had offered to supply funds, but she refused because of their relationship as lovers. She prefers a business transaction with her old friend. Now twenty, she is anxious to sail and get on with her career.

PART VI: KRONBORG

Ten years later, Dr. Archie, now a mining executive and genial widower, comes to New York to hear Thea sing Elsa in Lohengrin. He has not seen her since she left for Europe. She did not even return during her gallant mother's last illness.

On stage she is brilliant and gracious but seems harder. After her performances, she is tired and worn, almost dazed. He learns that she almost married an opera star abroad, but the latter's wife made impossible demands. Visiting Thea with Fred and a young accompanist, Landry, he sees that she is almost wholly absorbed in her work. He is also amazed at her resilience when she is called suddenly to substitute for an ailing performer. She is subsequently applauded when she again magnificently interprets the role of Sieglinde in *Die Walküre*, this time before a packed opera house with such old friends in the audience as Fred, Archie, the Harsanyis, and even Spanish Johnny, now in town with the circus.

EPILOGUE

Aunt Tillie, the last Kronborg in Moonstone, basks in Thea's glory. She once spent a glorious week with her in Kansas City, and her husband, Fred Ottenburg, was most kind. She is pleased, but not surprised, that Thea has sung before the King of England, and finds that other quiet folk also enjoy hearing of this Colorado girl's triumphs in the great world beyond their borders.

Comment:

Published in 1915, *The Song of the Lark* is the longest and most detailed in development of Willa Cather's novels. Moonstone is largely Red Cloud, and Thea at times resembles the author. She, too, was talented, independent, and determined. Her friend, Dr. G. E. McKeeby, served as model for Dr. Archie; her music teacher Professor Shindelmeisser became Wunsch; and Mrs. Kronborg is somewhat like Willa's mother. Moreover, she lived like Thea in an overcrowded house, and was much pleased with her own room.

For the portrait of Thea, however, Miss Cather drew also upon the career of the opera star Olive Fremstad, whom she much admired. Born in Sweden, the great diva was raised in a small Minnesota town, gave piano lessons as a girl, and had to struggle hard to achieve success.

Most critics point out that the earlier Moonstone sections and even those on Chicago are more interesting than the later ones in which Thea is seen as an established personage. Miss Cather herself agreed, admitting that she found most fascinating the young artist's efforts to escape from a hostile environment.

It has also been suggested that the romance with Fred lacks color and conviction.

The book does have memorable characterizations - Wunsch, Ray Kennedy, Spanish Johnny - and a genuine feeling for the beauty of the canyon country of the Southwest. This region will again figure in *The Professor's House* and *Death Comes for the Archbishop*. It shows, too, the author's impatience with narrow-minded small towns, her respect for such slighted groups as the Mexicans, and her sensitive understanding of the artistic temperament. She always admires the creative personality. But here she shows, too, the price paid to reach a high goal.

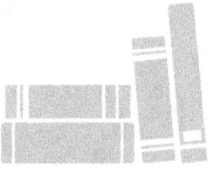

ONE OF OURS

....

Willa Cather received the Pulitzer Prize, in 1922, for *One of Ours*.

The Nebraska of *One of Ours* is a land of replaceable parts; a land where orchards seem a waste of time, when it is just as easy to go into town for fresh fruits. The people have lost touch with the land; they have become materialistic. Machines have brought about these changes. Machines also bring about an important change in Claude's life. When a passing truck frightens Claude's mules, he loses control of them and is thrown into barbed-wire. While he is recovering, Enid visits him everyday. He interprets her good-will calls as love and decides to marry her.

Enid, on the other hand, is quite compatible with machines. She handles a car very well, and, after her marriage, drives into surrounding towns almost every night working for prohibition, leaving Claude at home, alone.

Claude is spiritually renewed by World War I. It is an adventure to him, an adventure which he can share with men he likes and admires, an adventure into which he can channel all his energy and idealism.

His mother, who understood Claude better than anyone, realizes that it was better that Claude died during the war, that he died believing in something. She has seen heroes return home, only to be disappointed with life, many of them eventually killing themselves. Mrs. Wheeler was glad that Claude did not have to face that disappointment.

Willa Cather had seen the changes brought about by World War I. She had seen the industrialization that took over the land; she had seen the young heroes return home, only to become unhappy. Cather believed that it was better to be destroyed by war, than by disillusion.

Willa Cather received much criticism for the second half of *One of Ours*. In a time when many men who had fought in World War I were writing about it, such as Hemingway, a lot of people resented Cather's romanticism. They felt that she had never been close enough to the War to be able to write about it.

One of Ours is a romantic novel. It is the story of man versus the world . . . a world which is unjust.

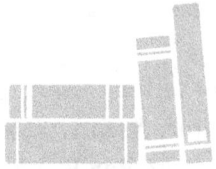

DEATH COMES FOR THE ARCHBISHOP

Written in 1927, *Death Comes for the Archbishop* was an experimental book for Willa Cather. She received inspiration for the novel from *The Life of The Right Reverend Joseph P. Machebeuf*, by Father Howlett.

Fathers Latour and Vaillant are simple, pious men who triumph over the rough, unexplored country and its society. The two priests have been friends since they were at the seminary. They are opposites who blend beautifully. Father Latour is a quiet, gentle thinker; Father Vaillant is friendly, a man of action.

The Indian and Mexican customs are described throughout the book. Like the early pioneers of Cather's earlier novels, the Indians and Mexicans show a love and understanding of nature. Father Latour is quick to note that, while a white man goes to great lengths to leave his mark on the land he travels, the Indian goes to great lengths to leave no marks, to leave the land as he found it. The Indians live harmoniously with nature; the white man fights nature.

Father Latour also has a great affinity to nature. He observes with pleasure the cultivation of New Mexico, the cool, dry wind of the country. He picks the spot for his cathedral because of its natural, beautiful surroundings.

Death Comes for the Archbishop is a story of two men who accomplish their goals in life by living close to God, his land, and his people.

When death comes for the archbishop, he dies peacefully and gracefully, as he has lived.

Death Comes for the Archbishop was an experimental novel for Willa Cather. It has no standardized plot or story. A novel of tales within a tale, it has no suspense or drama. It is a gentle narrative, full of **imagery** and atmosphere.

Death Comes for the Archbishop is a romantic-realistic novel, a tribute to the times when men like Fathers Latour and Vaillant lived.

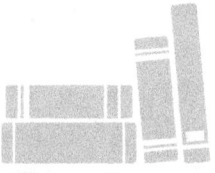

TOPICS FOR FURTHER RESEARCH

Satiric Humor in the Cather Novels

How the Cather Novels are "Unfurnished"

Imagery in *My Antonia*

Willa Cather's Independent Women

Social Criticism in the Cather Novels

My Antonia as an Unconventional Novel

Willa Cather's View of the Midwestern Farm

Lessons from the Past

How the Immigrants Fared

Willa Cather and the American Dream

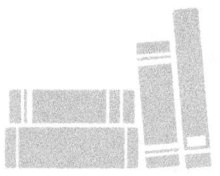

BIBLIOGRAPHY

WORKS BY WILLA CATHER

Novels

Alexander's Bridge (1912)

O Pioneers! (1913)

The Song of the Lark (1915)

My Antonia (1918)

One of Ours (1922)

A Lost Lady (1923)

The Professor's House (1925)

My Mortal Enemy (1926)

Death Comes for the Archbishop (1927)

Shadows on the Rock (1931)

Lucy Gayheart (1935)

Sapphira and the Slave Girl (1940)

Collections Of Short Stories

The Troll Garden (1905)

Youth and the Bright Medusa (1920)

Obscure Destinies (1932)

December Night (1933)

The Old Beauty and Others (1948)

Verse

April Twilights (1923)

Collections Of Essays

Not Under Forty (1936)

Willa Cather on Writing (1949)

The Houghton Mifflin Company published a "Library Edition" of the works of Willa Cather in 13 volumes during the years 1937 to 1941. Essay and short story collections have appeared since then, and there are now attractive paperback editions of such works as *My Antonia, O Pioneers!*, and *The Song of the Lark*.

Full-Length Biographical And Critical Studies

Bennet, Mildred R. *The World of Willa Cather.* New York: Dodd, Mead, & Company, 1951. A second edition with notes and index has since been published by Bison Books, University of Nebraska Press, 1961.

Bloom, Edward A., and Lillian D. Bloom. *Willa Cather's Gift of Sympathy.* Carbondale: Southern Illinois University Press, 1962.

Bonham, Barbara. *Willa Cather.* Pennsylvania: Chilton, 1970.

Brown, E.K. *Willa Cather: A Critical Biography*, completed by Leon Edel. New York: Alfred A. Knopf, 1953.

Brown, Marion M., and Ruth Crone. *Willa Cather: The Woman and Her Works.* New York: Charles Scribner and Sons, 1971.

Daiches, David. *Willa Cather: A Critical Introduction.* Ithaca, New York: Cornell University Press, 1951.

Giannone, Richard. *Music in Willa Cather's Fiction.* Lincoln: University of Nebraska Press, 1968.

Randall, John H. *The Landscape and the Looking Glass: Willa Cather's Search for Values.* Boston: Houghton Mifflin Company, 1960.

Schroeter, James Marvin. *Willa Cather and Her Critics.* Ithaca, New York: Cornell University Press, 1967.

Sergeant, Elizabeth Shepley. *Willa Cather: A Memoir.* New York: J.B. Lippincott Company, 1953.

Slote, Bernice. *The Kingdom of Art.* Willa Cather's First Principles and Critical Statements 1893-1896. Lincoln: University of Nebraska Press, 1968.

_____. *Willa Cather: A Pictorial Memoir.* Lincoln: University of Nebraska Press, 1973.

Van Ghent, Dorothy. *Willa Cather.* Minneapolis: University of Minnesota Press, 1964.

Woodress, James Leslie. *Willa Cather: Her Life and Art.* New York: Pegasus, 1970.

Shorter Critical Pieces

Auchincloss, Louis. "Willa Cather," in *Pioneers and Caretakers: A Study of Nine American Woman Authors.* Minneapolis: University of Minnesota Press, 1965, pp. 92-122.

Connolly, Francis X. "Willa Cather: Memory as Muse," in *Fifty Years of the American Novel: A Christian Appraisal.* ed. Harold C. Gardiner, S.J. New York: Charles Scribner and Sons, 1952, pp. 69-87.

Geismar, Maxwell. "Willa Cather: Lady in the Wilderness," in *The Last of the Provincials.* New York: Hill and Wang, 1959, pp. 153-220.

Kazin, Alfred. "Willa Cather and Ellen Glasgow," in *Literature in America*, ed. Philip Rahv. New York: Meridian Books, World Publishing Company, 1962, pp. 308-322.

Lee, R. E. "The Westerners: Willa Cather," in *From West to East*, Urbana, Illinois: University of Illinois Press. 1966, pp. 112-135.

Miller, J. E. "Wharton and Cather: The Quest for Culture," in *Quests Surd and Absurd.* Chicago, Illinois: University of Chicago Press, 1967, pp. 76-92.

Porter, Katherine A. "Reflections on Willa Cather," in *The Collected Essays and Occasional Writings of Katherine Anne Porter.* New York: Delacorte Press 1971, pp. 29-39.

Slote, Bernice. "Willa Cather," in *Fifteen Modern American Authors*, ed., Jackson R. Bryer. Durham, North Carolina: Duke University Press, 1969, pp. 23-62.

Trilling, Lionel. "Willa Cather," in *After the Genteel Tradition*, ed. Malcolm Cowley. Gloucester, Mass.: Peter Smith, 1959, pp. 52-63.

Van Doren, Carl. "Willa Cather," in *The American Novel*, 1789-1939. New York: The Macmillan Company, 1960, pp. 281-293.

Wagenknecht, Edward. "Willa Cather and the Lovely Past," in *Cavalcade of the American Novel.* New York: Holt, Rinehart and Winston, 1963, pp. 319-338.

www.ingramcontent.com/pod-product-compliance
Lightning Source LLC
LaVergne TN
LVHW011711060526
838200LV00051B/2853